It Runs in the Family

A comedy

Ray Cooney

Samuel French — London
New York - Toronto - Hollywood

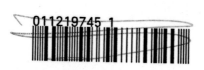

CHARACTERS

Dr David Mortimore
Dr Mike Connolly
Rosemary Mortimore
Dr Hubert Bonney
Matron
Sir Willoughby Drake
Jane Tate
Sister
Leslie
Police Sergeant
Bill
Mother

The action of the play takes place in the Doctors' Common Room of St Andrew's Hospital, London

ACT I   Three days before Christmas. 10.45 a.m.
ACT II Immediately following

Time—the present

COPYRIGHT INFORMATION

(See also page ii)

IT RUNS IN THE FAMILY

First performed on November 21st, 1987 at the Yvonne Arnaud Theatre, Guildford, with the following cast:

Dr David Mortimore	John Quayle
Dr Mike Connolly	Peter Blake
Dr Hubert Bonney	Ray Cooney
Matron	Charmian May
Sir Willoughby Drake	Dennis Ramsden
Jane Tate	Una Stubbs
Rosemary Mortimore	Wanda Ventham
Leslie	Ian McCurrach
Sister	Ginni Barlow
Police Sergeant	Bill Pertwee
Bill	Derek Royle

Directed by Ray Cooney
Designed by Douglas Heap
Lighting designed by Paul Franklin

It was subsequently presented at The Playhouse, London, on 17th August 1992, by Lee Menzies and Ashley Herman by arrangement with the Theatre of Comedy in association with Charles Kelman. The cast was as follows:

Dr David Mortimore	John Quayle
Dr Mike Connolly	Michael Fenner
Rosemary Mortimore	Wanda Ventham
Dr Hubert Bonney	Ray Cooney
Matron	Jacqueline Clarke
Sir Willoughby Drake	Dennis Ramsden
Jane Tate	Sandra Dickinson
Sister	Jennifer Hill
Leslie	William Harry
Police Sergeant	Windsor Davies
Bill	Henry McGee
Mother	Doris Hare

Directed by Ray Cooney
Decor by Douglas Heap
Lighting by Mark Doubleday

IT RUNS IN THE FAMILY

'Ray Cooney's new farce is deftly organized, well oiled and runs beautifully. A must for the bruised in spirit and the young at heart.' John Peter, *Sunday Times*

'He builds the comic momentum to a point near delirium... By the end of an hilarious evening ... I was definitely rocking in my seat.' Michael Arditti, *Evening Standard*

'Cooney hangs a carefully constructed mobile of lying cover-ups and set it sublimely and hilariously spinning.' Kenneth Hurren, *Mail on Sunday*

'Thoroughly enjoyable.' Kirsty Milne, *Sunday Telegraph*

'There's no doubt about its staying power at the Playhouse. Judging by the first night audience reaction, it will probably notch up a year or three.' Michael Darvell, *What's On*

'My glasses steamed up with laughter.' Maureen Paton, *Daily Express*

'Critic-proof, recession proof, possibly even bullet-proof: the Ray Cooney farce doesn't run for weeks, it runs for years. It's impossible not to enjoy such a well executed romp.' James Christopher, *Time Out*

'A master of farcical arts.' Michael Billington, *Guardian*

'Cooney's frantic tale tickles the funny bone quite shamelessly.' Clive Hirschorn, *Sunday Express*

'A Rolls-Royce of a farce.' Charles Spencer, *Daily Telegraph*

It Runs in the Family — The Playhouse production

Photograph by Reg Wilson

Other plays by Ray Cooney
published by Samuel French Ltd

Out of Order
Run for Your Wife!
Two Into One
Why Not Stay for Breakfast? (written
with Gene Stone)
Wife Begins at Forty (written with
Arne Sultan and Earl Barret)

ACT I

The action of the play takes place in the Doctors' Common Room on the third floor of St Andrew's Hospital, London

It is an old-fashioned, comfortable room reflecting the occupants' profession. There are double swing doors UL leading to a corridor and another pair of double swing doors DR leading to another corridor. A single door UR leads to the toilet/bathroom and a similar door DL leads on to a landing. There are large windows UC with a panoramic view of London in the background. In front of the window is a window seat. There is a 'food and drinks' sideboard over which there is a mirror along the centre of the L wall. A small desk and chair are ULC. A telephone is on the desk. Upstage of the doors DR there are some hooks on which are hanging overcoats, scarves, jackets, etc. Two unmatching armchairs of differing size are situated DLC and DRC. There are various bits and pieces of medical origin scattered around the room. Intermittently snow will be seen falling outside the window

The CURTAIN rises on a snowy morning three days before Christmas. The room is decorated for Christmas and there is a Christmas tree below the UL swing doors. The clock above the swing doors UL shows 10:45 and the time advances with the action of the play

David is discovered writing at the desk. He is in his early fifties, charming and slightly pompous. He is wearing dark trousers and a waistcoat (his jacket is hanging on the back of his chair). He rises and checks his written speech. After a moment he addresses an unseen audience

David "... And so at a time when the world is looking to the medical profession for guidance, for assurance, for higher standards of techniques and professionalism and dedication and — er— (*He checks with his paper*) learning — I ask you, my fellow neurologists, my colleagues from far and wide — (*he points to parts of the audience*) from Australia — Canada — Pakistan — Bulgaria. I ask you to recall the words of the Hippocratic Oath ——

Dr Mike Connolly, carrying a plate of mince pies, enters through the door DL. *Mike is an exuberant doctor in his late twenties*

Mike (*calling off*) I'll carve the turkey and tell that butcher to save his mistakes for surgery.

He chuckles and bangs the door shut. David glares at him as Mike turns and sees him

Mike 'Morning, Dr Mortimore. Have a mince pie?
David I'm busy, Connolly.
Mike Aren't we all, sir? Three days to Christmas and we're only just starting rehearsals for the pantomime. Did Sister Henderson leave a set of Victorian costumes here for me?
David I'm trying to learn this, do you mind?
Mike Is that your Father Christmas speech for the patients?
David (*flatly*) It's my lecture for the Conference this morning.
Mike (*dismissively*) Oh, that?

Mike looks in the dresser for costumes

David It may interest you to know, Connolly, that my fellow neurologists — from as far afield as Iceland and Japan — consider it worthwhile making this journey to London.

Mike crosses to the window seat and opens it

Mike I should think they do. All expenses paid and a week at the Savoy.

David goes back to his speech. Mike has found the costumes, and during the ensuing dialogue he is sorting them out and, at the same time, eating a mince pie

Here we are. What time are you on?
David (*tersely*) Twelve o'clock.
Mike (*ominously*) One hour and fourteen minutes to high noon. Good luck.
David Thank you.
Mike You nervous?
David Yes!

Mike Well, don't worry, with two hundred neurologists out there you won't go short of tranquilizers.

David gives him a cold look and then returns to his speech

David " — for higher standards of techniques, professionalism, dedication and learning, I ask you, my fellow neurologists ...

Rosemary Mortimore enters from DL. *She is an attractive woman a little younger than David. She is very smartly dressed and wearing a top coat*

... my colleagues from far and wide ... "

Rosemary Sorry to trouble you, David ——

David (*exasperated*) Rosemary, darling!

Rosemary I need some change for the parking meter.

David I'm trying to work on my speech. (*He looks for change in his pocket*)

Rosemary Sorry, sweetheart, but I'm double parked. Good-morning, Dr Connolly.

Mike is now trying on a Long John Silver pirate's coat

Mike 'Morning, Mrs Mortimore. You here for the Lecture?

Rosemary You bet. I couldn't miss my husband's big day, could I?

David Your husband's big day will be a fiasco if I don't know my speech.

Rosemary Last night you knew it backwards.

Mike I say, that will be a novelty. Have a mince pie.

Rosemary No thank you.

Mike They're very good. Made by the sister in charge of contagious diseases.

Rosemary I'll wait till Christmas Day.

David Connolly, have you any change on you? (*To Rosemary*) You're very early, aren't you, Rosemary?

Rosemary Sir Willoughby said something about you and I welcoming the delegates into the lecture hall.

Mike (*producing coins*) A couple of quid OK?

Rosemary (*taking the money*) Lovely. David will pay you back. (*To David*) If I don't get another chance, darling, "Good Luck".

David Thank you, dear.

Rosemary You'll be wonderful.

David Thank you!
Rosemary Are you nervous?
David Yes!
Rosemary I'll see you in the lecture hall, Dr Connolly.

Mike moves downstage holding a fairy costume and a wand

Mike No, I've got more important things to do than that.
David Thank you, Connolly.
Mike I'm rehearsing for the Boxing Day pantomime.
Rosemary Ah, well, that is important, of course. Are you in it this year, David?
David (*tersely*) In what, dear?
Mike The St Andrew's pantomime.
David Connolly, all I'm interested in at the moment is the Ponsonby Lecture and my two hundred fellow neurologists.
Rosemary Actually, darling, I think the two hundred neurologists might be happier if you gave them the pantomime instead of the lecture.

Rosemary smiles and exits DL

Mike laughs. David gives him a cold look

David Connolly, why don't you wave that and disappear?

Mike returns to his costumes and David to his speech

"I — I ask you, my fellow neurologists ——"

Dr Hubert Bonney enters from DR. *He is an insignificant but enthusiastic man in his early fifties*

Hubert Ah, there you are, David!
David God!

Hubert removes his white jacket and takes his suit jacket from the pegs DR

Hubert 'Morning, Mike.
Mike 'Morning, Dr Bonney. Are you all right for today's rehearsal?

Hubert Oh, yes, I'll be there. (*To David.*) Just thought I'd wish you good luck.

David Thank you, Hubert.

Hubert Big day, eh?

David Yes.

Hubert You nervous?

David Yes! But with two hundred neurologists out there I won't be short of tranquilizers, will I?

Hubert (*innocently*) Would you like a tranquilizer?

David No! Hubert, I'm trying to work on my lecture.

Hubert Ah. I'll let you get on with it then.

David Thank you.

David returns his attention to his papers

Hubert Are you memorizing the whole speech?

David I'm trying to!

Hubert (*impressed*) I say! I'm finding it difficult enough remembering my first line in Dr Connolly's melodrama. I'm the villain, aren't I, Mike?

Mike You are indeed.

Hubert I have to come on and say to Matron — she's the heroine — I have to say, "Ahoy in front and avast behind." (*To Mike.*) Are you sure that's a big laugh?

Mike A belter.

Hubert Yes. I don't quite see why.

David Hubert, shouldn't you be on your rounds?

Hubert Just finished. Well, what a day, eh? I never thought when we were students here you'd be up on that rostrum one day delivering the Ponsonby Lecture.

David If you don't stop nattering I won't be delivering anything.

Hubert Of course. My dear fellow. Would you like me to make you a nice cup of tea?

David No, thank you.

Mike puts a red hat on David's head

Mike (*as he does so*) There's your Father Christmas hat. You couldn't cope with him and play a dead body in my melodrama, could you?

David Just take your costumes and go.

Mike I suggested we borrow a real body from the mortuary but Dr Saunders wouldn't have it.

Matron enters UL *wheeling a hospital trolley on top of which is what looks like a body covered in a sheet. Matron is a large lady*

Matron Excuse me, gentlemen.

David People are in and out of here like a stomach pump.

Matron Oh, we are a grumpy Father Christmas, aren't we?

David Matron, this is supposed to be the Doctors' Common Room.

Matron Correct, and I'm taking a shortcut.

Mike Of course. Quite right. Don't apologize, Matron.

Matron I wasn't going to.

Hubert (*referring to the trolley*) Matron, is that anyone we know?

Matron (*lifting the sheet*) The patients' Christmas presents. (*She reveals a trolley full of wrapped Christmas packages*)

Hubert Very good. I'll give you a hand, shall I? (*He pushes the trolley* DR)

Matron Thank you, Dr Bonney. We're keeping them in the mortuary until Christmas Day.

Mike And don't forget, Matron, rehearsals are about to commence.

Matron Rehearsals.

Hubert Dr Connolly's melodrama.

Matron I haven't got time for that.

Hubert (*as they go*) Matron, perhaps you could explain the significance of "Ahoy in front and avast behind"?

Matron gives Hubert a severe look and they exit DR *with the trolley*

Mike (*to David*) I hope I'm not going to have to explain all the bad jokes to Dr Bonney.

David Connolly, will you either be quiet or go and rehearse.

Mike (*putting a lady's bonnet on his head*) My, but you're so masterful!

Sir Willoughby Drake enters from DL. *He is an elderly, stern gentleman*

Drake Is Dr Mortimore anywhere ...?

He stops on seeing Mike wearing the bonnet

Who are you, sir?

Mike Dr Connolly, sir. One of the housemen.

Drake Is that the headgear you're wearing this year?

Mike Mm? Oh, no, Sir Willoughby. Rehearsing for the pantomime. Would you care for a mince pie, sir?

Drake (*interrupting*) Get out. I want to speak to Dr Mortimore.

Drake pours himself a stiff whisky as Mike collects up his costumes

Mike Yes, of course. May I take this opportunity to wish you a very Happy Christmas, Sir Willoughby?

Drake Clear off!

Mike starts to go, but returns

Mike I don't suppose you'd like to play the fairy?

Drake glares at him

Mike exits DR

David Good-morning, Sir Willoughby.

Drake (*impatiently*) Yes, yes, yes. Now, Mortimore, I don't have to emphasize the importance of the Annual Ponsonby Lecture ——

David Certainly not, Sir Willoughby.

Drake Don't interrupt, please.

David Sorry.

Drake As Chairman of the Board of Governors and past Head Surgeon of St Andrew's I consider that I'm in a unique position ——

David You most certainly are. Do sit down, sir.

Drake (*ignoring this*) A unique position when it comes to selecting the Ponsonby Lecturer. This year, Mortimore, I don't think it's any secret that you were not the first choice for the role.

David (*lightly*) Well, I'd heard rumours that I wasn't top of the list.

Drake You were bottom. However, beggars can't be choosers. Against my advice Neurology was designated this year's subject. You're the senior specialist here. *Ipso facto* — you're delivering the Ponsonby Lecture. (*He tops his glass up*)

David I won't let you down, Sir Willoughby.

Drake God help you, if you do. Does your speech contain any references to the present government?

David Definitely not, sir.

Drake Well, put some in, you damn fool.

David Oh, right. Any references in particular?

Drake Complimentary ones, for heaven's sake. The Junior Health Minister's attending the lecture and we need a new scanner.

David (*writing*) Complimentary references it will be, sir.

Drake And plead poverty.

David Poverty, right.

Drake But don't let those overseas medicos think we're hard up.

David Right. Not hard up but plead poverty.

Drake And keep it brief. Neurology numbs the brain. See me in my office in five minutes. I'd better vet this speech of yours.

David Thank you, sir. Most kind. Five minutes.

Drake (*hesitating, fractionally*) The Ponsonby Lecture could be the step up to Head Physician for you here.

David Well, of course, I hadn't even allowed myself to think that far ahead.

Drake Damn liar. You know full well there's a tradition at St Andrew's that the Ponsonby Lecture is practically a direct line to a knighthood.

David (*hoarsely*) Knighthood.

Drake Why do you think I got mine?

David (*innocently*) I've often wondered about that.

Drake Five minutes!

Drake exits DR

David immediately starts to address his unseen audience

David " — Fellow neurologists — we're fortunate in this country to — er — have more than sufficient funds to maintain a robust vigorous Health Service. However, I see that we have the Junior Minister for Health in our audience — and for him I'd like to plead poverty."

Jane's head appears round the door DL, *unseen by David. She is about forty, pretty and cuddly*

"Now, although I must be — er — brief — I would like to compliment the government on — er ——

Jane Excuse me ——

David (*jumping*) For heaven's sake.

Jane Sorry, I didn't mean ——

David (*interrupting*) This is the Doctors' Common Room.

Jane Yes, I know.

David Patients' Waiting Room is downstairs in the Main Hall.

Jane It's you I want to see, Dr Mortimore.

David The receptionist will make an appointment for you and I'm afraid you'll need a note from your GP.

Jane It's me, Dr Mortimore. Jane.

David (*blankly*) Jane? (*Suddenly realizing*) Good heavens! Nurse Tate.

Jane I didn't mean to give you a shock.

David Yes — no — well, — good heavens!

Jane It's been a long time. Over eighteen years.

David Good heavens! You don't look a day older.

Jane (*grinning*) Is that why you recognized me right away?

David Well, no *more* than a day. And you were always the prettiest on the ward.

Jane And that's what you said to all the nurses.

David Nonsense, you were the prettiest, and as far as I was concerned, the most efficient.

Jane As far as you were concerned, I was certainly the most accommodating.

David Nurse Tate, please! (*He hastily closes the door* DL) I don't do — what we did — with all the nurses.

Jane Just some of them, eh?

David Miss Tate — Jane — I'm a very happily married man.

Jane You were a very happily married man eighteen years ago.

David Yes, I was, and still am. Anyway, to the best of my recollection you were perfectly willing.

Jane Yes, of course. It was wonderfully naughty and romantic. Rolling around out there on the Sluice Room floor.

David Well, it's grand seeing you, after all this time.

Jane (*suddenly*) Oh God! May I sit down? My knees are knocking. (*She sits*)

David I'm a bit worried about the time actually. I'm delivering the Ponsonby Lecture this morning.

Jane (*suddenly rising*) I should have told you eighteen years ago.

David Told me what?

Jane Didn't you ever wonder why I suddenly left the hospital? Without even saying goodbye properly?

David Well, I remember thinking that it seemed a bit abrupt.

Jane I was expecting.

David Expecting what?

Jane After what we did what do you think I was expecting?

David Couldn't have been a raise. (*He chuckles at his joke*)

Jane I left the hospital to have a baby.

David (*still chuckling*) A baby! (*Suddenly realizing*) A baby?

Jane Yes!

David We had a baby?

Jane It was my fault. Stupid. A nurse getting herself pregnant.

David Hardly brilliant for a doctor, either. Do you mind if I sit down? (*He sits*)

Jane Can I get you anything?

David Like a cigar? (*Rising*) I can't sit down, I've got to see Sir Willoughby Drake in five minutes. (*Sitting*) And my wife will be back any moment ... (*Rising*) Oh, my God, my wife! (*Sitting*) This really is one hell of a ... (*He rises*) It might not be mine, of course, Miss Tate.

Jane It is. There wasn't anyone else.

David (*sitting*) Oh, good.

Jane I so nearly told you at the time, but then I thought there was no need to make a mess of your life as well. You were ambitious. Hoping to specialize.

David Miss Tate, this really is a very busy morning for me. Why have you suddenly decided to tell me after all this time?

Jane Because of Leslie.

David Leslie?

Jane That's our son.

David Our baby's a little boy, is he?

Jane Les is quite a big boy now.

David Yes, I suppose he would be.

Jane Well, I'd always told Leslie that his father's name was Tate. And that I was Mrs Tate.

David (*curtly*) That's very good.

Jane And that Mr Tate had died when Leslie was a tiny baby seventeen years ago.

David (*curtly*) Excellent.

Jane Climbing the Himalayas.

David Himalayas?

Jane I thought it was nice for a little boy to have a picture of his daddy as a sort of romantic hero.

David Fine.

Jane Then yesterday I told Les the truth.

David (*aghast*) You did what?

Jane It was his eighteenth birthday.

David And that was his present, was it?

Jane No. I'd come round to thinking that when he was eighteen he should know the real truth about his father.

David (*mortified*) Miss Tate!

Jane I didn't say it was *you* exactly. I mean not by name.

David What *did* you say exactly?

Jane Just that I'd had an affair with a young doctor here in St Andrew's when I was a trainee nurse and that he was already married.

David That was all right.

Jane No it wasn't. I didn't appreciate what it would mean to Les. All day yesterday he went on about it. I'd never seen him like this. Laughing and crying.

David God!

Jane And as it was his birthday, we'd had some champagne. I don't think that helped.

David But you didn't actually tell him my name.

Jane No, but this morning the poor boy was in dreadful condition. He'd taken some pills last night because he couldn't sleep but they hadn't worked so he'd finished off the champagne.

David Good God!

Jane Washing down with half a bottle of gin.

David Champagne, gin and pills?!

Jane Yes.

David If you'd done that eighteen and a half years ago we wouldn't have had this problem today.

Jane He was quite hysterical. He seemed to think it was all your fault.

David My fault?

Jane For deserting me and leaving him fatherless.

David Dammit, I didn't even know about "Les" until five minutes ago.

Jane He's very confused.

David *He's* confused?!

Jane If you could have seen him this morning. I should have insisted he stayed in bed. He's only got a learner driving licence, you see.

David (*after a pause*) A learner driving licence?

Jane He said he'd made up his mind to come to the hospital and find out who his father was.

David (*aghast*) What?!

Jane And before I could stop him he jumped in my car and drove off.

David Oh, my God!

Jane I got in a taxi and followed.

David Wretched boy!

Jane He's downstairs at Reception.

David Reception?!

Jane Don't you see? Instead of his father's bones lying in some crevasse halfway up the Himalayas, you're actually alive and available.

David Oh, no I'm not! I may be alive, Miss Tate, but I'm not available. I'm delivering the Ponsonby Lecture at twelve o'clock.

Jane Just see him for five minutes.

David I can't! Sir Willoughby Drake is waiting to vet my speech! Give me your telephone number. I'll try to ring you this afternoon.

Jane That's no good.

David It's the best I can do. Just get Leslie out of St Andrew's now.

Jane I can't.

David You must!

Jane I can't! He's with the police sergeant who arrested him.

David Police sergeant?

Jane Drunk in charge, driving while unqualified, exceeding the speed limit and no insurance.

David sits and holds his head

Jane And assaulting an officer.

Hubert enters from DR

Hubert Ah, David ——

David Hubert, not now!

Hubert Sir Willoughby says ... (*To Jane*) Excuse me. (*To David*) Sir Willoughby says he's expecting you in his office.

David I'll be with him in a baby — *maybe* I'll be with him.

Hubert I think he wants to see you before the lecture.

David Go and tell him I'm coming.

Hubert Well, I'm a bit involved at the moment. Rehearsing for the melodrama. "Ahoy in front and avast behind." Connolly explained the joke to me.

He chuckles and includes Jane. Hubert stops chuckling

Good heavens! (*To David*) It's Nurse Tate!

David (*hesitating a second*) I beg your pardon?

Hubert It's Nurse Tate, surely?

David (*hesitating*) That's right, it's Nurse Tate. I didn't know you knew her, Hubert.

Hubert (*astonished*) Didn't know I ... ? We were all here together. You two were always larking around. (*He chuckles innocently*)

David (*protesting*) I don't know that we were.

Hubert Yes! Playing silly tricks on one another. In and out of the Sluice Room. (*Admiring Jane*) Marvellous! Wonderful to see you.

Jane Wonderful to see you, too, Dr Bonney.

Hubert You look super, Nurse Tate. Jane, wasn't it?

Jane That's right.

Hubert Yes, Jane Tate. Lovely! (*To David*) I must say this is a terrific Christmas present she's given me.

David Yes, she's given me one, too.

Hubert (*admiring Jane*) Super!

Jane You haven't changed, Dr Bonney.

Hubert Well ... (*Indicating his hair*) Not much up top these days.

David There was never much in the first place.

Hubert (*chuckling at David's 'joke'; to Jane*) Well, well, well. How long is it?

David Eighteen years.

Hubert Eighteen years!

Jane (*flatly*) And nine months.

Hubert (*to Jane*) So, are you here on business or pleasure, Jane?

David ⎱ (*together*) ⎰ Pleasure.
Jane ⎰   ⎱ Business.

David Half and half. She came to wish us a Happy Christmas — that's the pleasure — and the business was to see if we had any vacancies — which we haven't.

Hubert We're desperately short of nurses.

David Young ones, yes. (*To Jane*) I've already explained that, haven't I? No vacancies for old nurses. Sorry you've got to dash and don't forget to stop off in the Main Hall on your way out. Take your little basket with you.

Hubert (*to Jane*) Surely she can stop and have a Christmas drink with us.

David She doesn't drink.

Hubert If I remember correctly, she did in the old days.

David There's a lot of things she did in the old days that she's regretting now.

Hubert (*chuckling*) The parties we used to have. We hardly found time for the patients. (*To Jane*) And I bet you managed to hook yourself a handsome husband.

Jane Well ——

David (*quickly*) Yes, she did actually.

Hubert I thought so. (*To Jane*) What's he do for a living?

David He's dead.

Hubert Oh, dear.

David Jane doesn't want to talk about her private life, Hubert. Very sad. She's just told me her husband fell while climbing the Himalayas.

Hubert Oh, how tragic. (*To Jane*) And when —— ?

David (*interrupting*) A long time ago.

Hubert Oh. (*To Jane*) And do you have any —— ?

David (*interrupting*) No, she doesn't! She's told me all about everything. No children and definitely not a son. No family at all. She's had a rotten life. I've just heard the whole story and it brought tears to my eyes.

Hubert Dear, oh dear.

David (*moving Hubert towards the swing door* R) Hubert, you're going to be late for your rehearsals. Off you go.

Hubert (*to Jane*) You should stay for David's lecture!

Jane (*brightly*) Well, I was just thinking I might do that actually.

David And then she remembered she couldn't. She's got Christmas shopping to do for the family.

Hubert I thought she didn't have any family.

David She's got a lot of very good friends who've become family.

David bundles Hubert out DR

Hubert exits

David (*collecting Jane's hat, coat and handbag*) Now! What's your telephone number?

Jane 674 3105.

David (*writing*) 674 3105.

Jane But what about Les?

David I'll do my best to ring you.

Jane But what about the sergeant?

David I'll do my best to ring him as well. Wait a minute. What does he know so far?

Jane Nothing about you. Leslie's just told him what *he* knows. That his father's a doctor here.

David Good.

Jane But the sergeant says he doesn't care who Leslie's father is. He wants Leslie to accompany him to the police station for a breathalyzer test.

David That's a good idea.

Jane But Leslie says he has the right to be accompanied by his father.

David Bloody know-all!

Jane So the sergeant let me come up here to see if you were available.

David Well, I'm not. Now you tell Leslie, if he doesn't accompany the sergeant to the police station he'll get himself arrested. (*He opens the door* DL) And if I make a mess-up of my lecture, it'll be thanks to *Master Leslie.*

Rosemary appears in the doorway DL

(*Quickly, for Rosemary's benefit, to Jane*) Yes, thank you, *Mrs Lesley.* Very pleased that I was able to see you, Mrs — er — Lesley. (*To Rosemary*) Hello, darling! (*Introducing Jane*) Darling, this is Mrs — er ——

Jane (*grinning*) Mrs *Lesley.*

David Lesley, yes. (*Introducing Rosemary*) And this is my wife, Mrs — er — er ——

Rosemary (*flatly*) Mortimore.

David Yes. Mrs Mortimore.

He embraces a surprised Rosemary. Behind Rosemary's back, David indicates for Jane to go. Jane smiles and shakes her head

(*To Rosemary*) Well, darling, what have you been up to?

Rosemary (*surprised*) I've been parking the car.

David Great, keep it up, darling.

He embraces her again and once more indicates for Jane to go. Jane shakes her head and sits on chair L. *David breaks the embrace*

Well!

Rosemary Are you on the staff here, Mrs Lesley?

Jane Actually, no.

David No. Mrs Lesley's — er — visiting. Yes. She's visiting her husband. He's a patient here. Yes, Mr — er ——

Jane Lesley.

David Thank you, yes. Mr Lesley's in — B Ward, did you say, Mrs Lesley?

Jane B Ward, yes.

David B Ward. Anyway, she was on her way home when she suddenly developed palpitations in the corridor. When I say she developed palpitations in the corridor I mean she was in the corridor when she developed palpitations ——

Rosemary I know what you mean, David.

Drake enters from DR *with an empty whisky glass in his hand*

Drake Dr Mortimore!

David Ah, Sir Willoughby, I'll be with you in a nappy — *happy*, to be with you.

Drake We said five minutes, Dr Mortimore.

David Indeed we did.

Drake That was ten minutes ago.

David Yes. This lady's Mrs Mortimore ——

Drake I know Mrs Mortimore!

Rosemary Good-morning, Sir Willoughby.

David And this lady's Mrs Do Dah.

Jane Mrs Lesley.

David Yes, Mrs Lesley. This is the Chairman of the Board of Governors, Sir Willoughby doo-dah — er — Drake. (*To Drake*) Slight problem. Mrs Lesley developed palpitations in the corridor. (*To Jane*) It's nothing to worry about.

Jane I'm getting less worried all the time, actually.

David Good. Yes. Allow me to get you a refill, Sir Willoughby.

Drake I don't want a ——

David (*pressing on*) I've got the speech all worked out, sir. The political angle, you know. A nice balance between poverty on the one hand and bankruptcy on the other.

David has poured a whisky for Drake and hands it to him

Drake (*to Rosemary*) Mrs Mortimore. When your husband has dealt with the palpitations in Mrs Lesley's corridor — perhaps you'd be good enough to bring him to my office to discuss the Ponsonby Lecture.

David Why not take my wife along now, sir, and discuss it with her first?

Drake reacts and then exits brusquely DR

Rosemary (*removing her coat*) You weren't as nervous as this when you left the house this morning. (*She hangs up her coat* DR)

David No, it hit me fairly recently. (*To Jane*) Well, you seem to have recovered nicely, Mrs Lesley. I'll see you to the lift.

Jane What about the *sergeant?*

Rosemary turns

David The sergeant ? Yes, well, tell the "sergeant" that your husband will just have to miss this year's Army Reunion. Mr Lesley is definitely not up to it. I'm sorry about this, darling. Mrs Lesley wants me to give a second opinion on Mr Lesley's condition. She's lost all confidence in the doctor here.

Rosemary Which doctor's that then?

David (*politely*) I beg your pardon?

Rosemary Who's her husband's doctor?

David Er — Dr Bonney.

Rosemary Hubert?

David Yes, Hubert.

Rosemary (*to Jane*) I can assure you that Dr Bonney is most competent.

David (*to Jane*) There you are, I told you that.

Jane You can spare five minutes, surely?

Rosemary (*interrupting*) You discuss your problem, whatever it is, with the sister on the ward.

Jane (*her voice rising*) I don't want to discuss it with the sister!

David Don't give way, Mrs Lesley, whatever you do. (*Pointedly*) Not in front of my wife. She has a very delicate disposition.

Rosemary You see Sir Willoughby about your speech. I'll take Mrs Lesley back to B Ward.

David That's not a good idea.

Rosemary (*to Jane*) And if we can't find Sister, we'll have a word with Dr Bonney.

David No, Mrs Lesley doesn't want to see Dr Bonney!

Rosemary He's in charge of her husband.

David She doesn't have any confidence in Dr Bonney!!

Rosemary Nonsense, Dr Bonney is an extremely able physician.

David Dr Bonney is a nincompoop!!!

Hubert enters from the swing doors R, *wearing his beard*

David reacts angrily

Hubert (*villainously*) Ha-ha! Somebody call? (*Seeing Rosemary*) Oh, good-morning, Mrs Mortimore. (*He removes his beard*)

Rosemary 'Morning, Hubert.

David (*gaily*) We're busy, Dr Bonney!

Hubert I'm after a black hat for the villain. (*To Jane*) Oh, you're still here, that's nice.

Rosemary She's very upset about her husband.

Hubert I'm sure she is.

David We all are.

Rosemary His name's Mr Lesley.

Hubert Mr Lesley? Is that so?

Rosemary He's in B Ward.

Hubert (*after a slight pause*) Who is?

David Mrs Lesley's husband!

Hubert Mrs Lesley's husband's dead.

Rosemary is taken aback and looks at Jane to see how she will receive this news. Jane hesitates and then emits a loud wail

Rosemary Oh, my God!

David (*angrily pulling Hubert away* DR) Really, Hubert!

Hubert What?

David That was cruel. Very, very cruel.

Hubert What was?

David Delivering the news like that.

Hubert The news?

Rosemary Yes, I must say, Dr Bonney, that was abrupt, to say the least. (*To Jane*) I'm so sorry. You'd better sit down.

David She can't sit down.

Jane (*realizing the strength of her position*) It might not be a bad idea to sit down. Just while I recover from the news.

She goes to sit but David pulls her up

David No! Sitting is very bad when you've had a shock. Fresh air. Lots of it and quickly.

Hubert (*to Jane*) What's happened then?

Rosemary Her husband's died, for heaven's sake.

Hubert I know. He fell in the Himalayas.

David (*to Jane*) Oh, God!

Rosemary Fell where?

Hubert In the Himalayas.

Rosemary How on earth did he get there?

Hubert Climbed, I suppose.

Rosemary But he was in St Andrew's five minutes ago.

Hubert Who was?

Rosemary Don't be so dense, Hubert. Mrs Lesley's husband.

Hubert (*bemused*) Mrs Lesley's husband was in —— ?

David (*interrupting, brightly.*) It's all right, Hubert. There's been a slight confusion. Mrs Lesley's husband *did* die — tragically — in a moutaineering expedition to the — er — Eastern Himalayas — that was her *first* husband. Her *second* husband — Mr Lesley ——

Rosemary (*relieved*) Oh, *second* husband.

Hubert (*surprised*) Second husband?

David Yes. Mr Lesley is at this moment a patient in our hospital.

Hubert (*surprised*) Is he?

David (*quickly*) Anyway, the good news is that the lady's husband in not deceased but making a splendid recovery.

Jane Oh, thank heavens!

David So she can leave St Andrew's with a light heart and a little basket.

Hubert (*to Jane*) So that's what you were doing here this morning, *visiting?*

David That's right and visiting hours are finished.

Hubert And I thought she called to see us.

David Hubert! Of course she called to see us. She would, wouldn't she? We're her husband's physicians, aren't we? (*To Rosemary*) Well, Hubert is.

Hubert Am I?

Rosemary Lesley. B Ward.

David It doesn't matter what ward he's in, Rosemary!

Hubert (*to Jane*) Lesley, you say.

Jane (*smiling at David*) Lesley, yes.

David We don't expect you to recall every patient you're responsible for, Dr Bonney.

Hubert I'm usually very good on names. Lesley. What's he in the hospital for?

David } (*together*) { Tests.
Jane } (*together*) { An operation.

David Mrs Lesley explained to me he was admitted for tests and we decided to operate.

Rosemary Oh, dear.

Hubert (*to David*) He came in for tests, you say?

David Yes, not serious. Suspected gout.

Hubert (*to Jane*) And we operated?

Jane (*flatly*) Yes. For piles.

David glares at her and she gives him a quick mischievous smile

Rosemary Good heavens!

Hubert (*amazed*) He was admitted with gout and we —— ?

David (*interrupting*) And we obviously discovered he had piles as well. We're thorough here, for God's sake, Dr Bonney. Now stop making such a fuss.

The phone rings. Hubert picks it up

Hubert Doctors' Common Room. . . . Mrs Tate? No, I don't think — oh, hang on a second. (*To Jane*) It's our receptionist downstairs. I think it might be for you. She's asking for Mrs Tate.

Jane Thank you. (*On the phone*) Hello?

Rosemary (*confused*) I thought her name was Mrs Lesley.

Jane (*on the phone*) This is Mrs Tate speaking.

David (*to Rosemary*) It is Mrs Lesley, but the fellow who came a cropper in the Himalayas was called Tate. So sometimes she's called Mrs Tate and sometimes she's called Mrs Lesley — so she was telling me.

Hubert Are you saying that Nurse Tate's first husband was also called Tate?

David Shut up, Hubert.

Rosemary (*confused*) Nurse Tate?

David Before Mrs Lesley married Mr Tate she was a nurse called Tate!

Hubert That's a hell of a coincid——

David Shut up, Hubert.

Jane (*on the phone*) Yes. I'll hang on for him.

David You really shouldn't be taking private calls in here, Mrs Lesley.

Jane The sergeant wants to talk to me.

David Well, go *downstairs* and talk to him.

Rosemary The sergeant?

David It's the one who's trying to get Mr Lesley to the army reunion.

Hubert (*surprised*) And the sergeant's called at our Reception?

David Yes, he's very keen!

Jane (*on the phone*) Yes, I am, but there's been a slight problem up here . . .

David (*to Hubert*) Dr Bonney, haven't you told Mr Lesley that he's in no fit state to attend regimental functions?

Hubert (*bemused*) No.

Jane (*on the phone*) Oh dear! (*To David*) Les is getting agitated again.

David (*growling*) Well, take him away.

Hubert Les?

David Yes. That's her little dog.

Hubert Little dog?

Jane (*on the phone*) Just look after him until I get there.

David (*to Rosemary*) It's neurotic, apparently.

Jane (*on the phone*) Very well, I'll be right down. (*She replaces the phone. To David*) I told you Leslie would crack up.

David Well, go and comfort him!

Hubert Leslie?

David Sometimes she calls the dog Les and sometimes she calls the dog Leslie!

Rosemary (*to Jane*) If you're called Lesley, isn't that rather confusing?

Jane (*flatly*) Only when my husband whistles. (*To David*) You definitely won't see him?

Rosemary Dr Mortimore's a physician, not a vet.

David I'll contact you later, Mrs Lesley. See the little fellow as soon as possible.

Rosemary Really, David.

David One has to put oneself out occasionally, darling. (*To Jane*) But whatever you do, don't let that neurotic animal get up here. What does the sign say outside the hospital, Dr Bonney?

Hubert St Andrew's.

David (*glaring at him*) It says "No Dogs Allowed".

Rosemary (*to Jane*) Dr Bonney will see you to the lift.

David (*giving Jane her coat and bag*) And no further. You've got to get back to your melodrama.

Hubert This way, my dear. (*He opens the door* DL)

Jane (*to David*) He'll probably go berserk, you realize that.

Hubert Have you ever considered castration?

David What a good idea!

Jane glares at David and storms out, followed by Hubert

(*Yelling after Hubert*) Just see her to the lift, Hubert! Don't go down-stairs. Damn dog's obviously vicious.

Rosemary What an extraordinary woman.

David Wasn't she just. You'd think she'd be more worried about her sick husband than the wretched dog. Well, let's go and have a word with Sir Willoughby and then I must prepare myself to meet two hundred neurologists.

Matron enters from the swing doors DR

Matron Excuse me, Dr Mortimore, Sir Willoughby Drake says he wants you to know he's getting very cross.

David We're on our way, Matron.

Rosemary Oh, Matron, what do you know about a Mr Lesley?

Matron Lesley?

Rosemary We believe he's in B Ward.

David It's nothing to do with us, darling.

Matron Lesley — can't say it rings a bell.

David (*tersely*) It doesn't matter, Matron.

Rosemary We don't want that woman making trouble. She looked as though she could be as neurotic as her dog.

Matron Dog?

David (*crossly*) Will you go about your business, Matron.

Rosemary Could you check, please, Matron. Mr Lesley came in with gout and was operated on for piles.

Matron (*surprised*) Came in with ——

David Gout, yes!

Matron And we operated for ——

David (*shouting*) Piles! Don't tell me you haven't heard of piles, Matron?!
A varicose condition of your rectum!
Matron Really!
Rosemary David!

Rosemary pulls David out DR

As Matron starts to move towards doors UL, *there is a knock on door* DL

Matron Come in.

Sister enters

Sister Oh. I was looking for Dr Mortimore.
Matron Not here, Sister, and I wouldn't bother him now.
Sister But he's Father Christmas and he'll need a list for the patient's
presents.
Matron See him after the Ponsonby Lecture, he's in a foul mood. Oh,
what do you know about a Mr Lesley?
Sister Lesley?
Matron Patient, B Ward.
Sister Don't recognize the name.
Matron Dr Mortimore wants to see him.
Sister What's Mr Lesley in for?
Matron Don't really know. Gout or piles, take your pick.
Sister I'll see what I can find out.

Sister exits DL. *David returns from* DR *and goes to collect his jacket*

David (*entering*) Forgot my jacket. God, what do I look like?
Matron (*coldly*) A varicose condition of your rectum.

Matron exits UL

David reacts and then picks up his speech

David "Poverty, bankruptcy..." (*He starts to move* DR *as the phone rings.
He hesitates and then lifts the receiver*) Dr Mortimore speaking. . . .
Miss Tate, are you still here?! . . . What do you mean, "When you got

down there, Leslie wasn't?" . . . Gone looking for you? How did he manage to get away from the sergeant? . . . Kicked him in the where? ... Oh, my God! . . . No, he hasn't come up here ——

The door DL *opens and Leslie appears. He is wearing jeans, a T-shirt and denim jacket. He also sports a punk hairstyle*

Leslie stops on seeing David and they look at each other for a moment. Leslie is out of breath and looks somewhat wild

(*On the phone*) I'd like to rephrase that last remark. (*He replaces the phone and stares at Leslie*)

Leslie Is this the Doctors' Common Room?

David Yes it is, and it's strictly for the use of the doctors.

Leslie ignores this remark and comes in, closing the door behind him

Leslie I'm looking for my mum.

David Your mum?

Leslie She's been up here talking to one of the doctors.

David Ah, yes! There was a lady on her way out when I arrived. She probably went down in the lift as you came up the stairs. (*He indicates for Leslie to leave*)

Leslie Are you one of the doctors in this place?

David (*hesitating, politely*) I beg your pardon?

Leslie (*raising his voice*) Are you a doctor here?

David Er — no. No, I'm not a doctor. No. (*Brightly*) I'm one of the patients, actually.

Leslie A patient?

David Yes. I'm recuperating. From gout and piles. Yes. And when you're recuperating they like you to do a little clerical work. Why not go and find your mother.

Leslie Rotten swine! (*He bangs his fist into the palm of his other hand*)

David Take it easy, young man!

Leslie He's a rotten swine!

David Who's a rotten swine?

Leslie My rotten dad.

David (*soothingly*) No he isn't.

Leslie How do *you* know?!

David Well, I'm sure he isn't. Dads aren't rotten.

Leslie Mine is. I'd like to thump him one.

David (*soothingly*) No, you wouldn't.

Leslie Yes I would! I'm going to stay here until I've seen every doctor in the hospital.

David You discuss it with your mother.

Leslie (*sitting*) I feel sick!

David God! Up you come.

Leslie I feel sick.

David If you feel sick, it'll be much nicer to be with your mother!

Leslie (*suddenly grabbing David*) I want to see my dad first. (*He falls to his knees*)

David I'll take you to the lift. (*He tries to get to the door* DL)

Leslie I didn't mean it, about thumping him.

David Just let go of me!

Drake enters from DR

Drake How much longer do you expect me to ... ? (*He stops on seeing Leslie, on his knees, clutching David*)

David (*after a pause*) This is private.

Drake reacts and then exits dumbly DR

(*To Leslie.*) Get a grip on yourself, for heaven's sake!

Leslie I feel sick!

Matron enters from UL

Matron Excuse me, I just wanted ... (*Seeing Leslie*) Oh.

David He's a bit upset, Matron.

Matron Upset?

David It's all right. His mother's in the hospital.

Matron (*to Leslie*) What ward's she in?

David I'll sort it out.

Leslie It's my dad I'm looking for.

Matron What ward's *he* in?

David I'm dealing with it, Matron! (*To Leslie*) It's all part of my recuperative clerical course.

Matron Recuperative clerical —— ?

David Just go on about your business, Matron!

Matron Well, actually, I came back to apologize for my rather offensive remark just now.

David It was nothing.

Matron It was very crude.

David (*taking her to the swing door* R) Most kind. Apologies accepted.

Matron Thank you, Doctor.

Matron exits R

David hesitates and then smiles sweetly at Leslie

Leslie (*to David*) She called you Doctor.

David Er — yes.

Leslie You said you were a patient.

David I am. I'm a patient who's a doctor. Of Divinity.

Leslie Divinity?

David (*laughing*) You probably don't know what a Doctor of Divinity is?

Leslie A clergyman.

David (*stopping laughing*) That's right. I'm a clergyman — recovering from gout and piles.

Leslie Why aren't you wearing a funny collar?

David I'm unorthodox. Now you go and find your mother.

Leslie I'm not going anywhere until I've seen my dad. (*He sits on the floor again*)

David But you can't stay here. The Doctors' Common Room is strictly private — unless you're a patient recuperating.

Leslie I don't care!

David Don't take that bloody attitude! (*Then sonorously*) My child.

Hubert enters from the door DL

Hubert Well, wasn't that nice seeing ... (*Seeing Leslie*) Oh. Who's this?

David He'll be all right. He's just lost his mother.

Hubert Oh dear, what did she die of?

David Never mind!

Hubert (*to Leslie*) The Lord giveth and the Lord taketh away.

David Never mind! (*To Hubert*) Help me take him downstairs.

Leslie (*to Hubert*) You leave me alone. And tell the vicar to leave me alone.

Hubert (*looking around*) The vicar?

Hubert looks at David, who also looks around

Leslie Yeah, get someone to put him back to bed.
Hubert (*to David*) Losing his mother's obviously affected him.
Leslie It's my dad I've lost!
Hubert Oh, not him as well!
David He's mislaid his father, that's all.
Hubert Oh, thank heavens for that. Two parents in one day would be awful.

Sisters enters from the door DL

Sister Excuse me, Dr Mortimore, it's about ——
David (*cheerfully, calmly*) Dr Mortimore — is not here.

Sister and Hubert look surprised

Sister I beg your pardon?
David Dr Mortimore is not here. Dr Mortimore *was* here — but Dr Mortimore is now enjoying his Christmas holidays.
Sister But I only wanted to ask if the patients' Christmas presents ——
David Then you'll have to ask Dr Mortimore after the holidays, won't you? Off with you.
Sister And I can't find a Mr Lesley in B Ward.
David Fine. We'll tell Dr Mortimore that when he returns. Off, off, off, off, off!

Sister backs out in confusion DL

Hubert Are you feeling all right, David?
David (*for Leslie's benefit*) No, I'm not, Doctor. And the sooner I'm allowed to return to the comfort of my bed in the sanctuary of my ward — the happier I shall be.
Hubert The comfort of ——
David My bed!
Hubert In the sanctuary of ——
David My ward! (*Growling*) Just help me pick him up.
Hubert (*patting Leslie's shoulder*) The Lord giveth and the Lord ——
David Shut up!

Rosemary enters from the swing doors R

Rosemary David ——!
David (*quickly dropping Leslie and going to Rosemary*) Yes, my darling?
Rosemary What on earth did you do to upset Sir Willoughby?
David Nothing.
Rosemary He said you can forget about any assistance from him with
    your speech and if you make any mistakes in your lecture, God help you.
David (*starting to push her out*) That's fair enough. You go and get a seat
    in the lecture hall.
Rosemary It doesn't start for another ... (*Seeing Leslie*) Who's that?
David He'll be all right.

Hubert, who has been comforting Leslie, joins them

Hubert (*to Rosemary, quietly*) His mother's just died.
David Hubert!
Rosemary Oh, no! (*Going to Leslie*) There, there, the Lord giveth and
    the ——
David Rosemary! (*He pulls Rosemary away*)
Leslie I want to see my dad!
David Stop that, for God's sake. (*Then sonorously*) For God's sake.
Leslie My dad's here somewhere, I know he is.
Rosemary Yes, you must be a comfort to your father now.

Leslie wails

David Rosemary! Leave this to us. Well, leave it to the doctor here. (*He
    indicates Hubert*)
Rosemary Was she a patient?
David Who?
Rosemary The boy's mother?
David No, she was D.O.A.
Hubert Oh dear.
Rosemary D.O.A.?
Hubert "Dead on arrival."
Rosemary What a morning! What did the poor woman die of?
David (*angrily interrupting*) Hit by a number 34 bus in Camden Town!
Hubert Dear oh dear.

Leslie (*to David*) I think I feel sick.
David Oh God — ! (*then smiling at Leslie*) — be with you.
Rosemary That'll be good for him. Into the bathroom.
Hubert Yes.

Hubert starts to lead Leslie to the bathroom. David pulls Rosemary L

David Rosemary, I really must insist you leave these hospital matters to the staff.

Mike enters from UL, *carrying the plate of mince pies, which has now been reduced to one mince pie*

Mike Come on, Dr Bonney, we're rehearsing.
Rosemary Ssh!
Mike He's the villain of my piece.

Rosemary points at Leslie who is being supported by Hubert

Rosemary His mother's just died.
Mike (*to Hubert, consolingly*) Oh, I'm so sorry to hear that, Dr Bonney.
David Connolly!
Mike (*to Hubert*) Still, she must have had a very good innings, eh, you're pushing on a bit.
Hubert (*pointing at Leslie*) *His* mother.
Mike Oh.
Rosemary She came C.O.D.

David, Hubert and Mike consider this

Hubert D.O.A., actually. (*To Mike*) Mike, help me get him into the bathroom, will you?
David Take him into one of the wards.
Rosemary Don't be silly. Get him into the bathroom.
Mike Have a mince pie, old lad.
Hubert He wants to be sick.
Mike This will bring that on a treat.
Leslie (*struggling*) I want to see my mother.
Rosemary It's all right. She's in better hands than ours now.

David Thank you, Rosemary!

Leslie She's gone downstairs.

Rosemary (*gently*) No, I'm sure she hasn't. She'll be up there somewhere. (*She looks heavenwards*)

Leslie No, she won't. The vicar definitely said she'd gone downstairs.

Rosemary looks to David who smiles and shrugs his shoulders

Rosemary What a thing for a vicar to say.

Hubert The boy needs his father here.

David No he doesn't!

Leslie Yes I do! (*He sits determinedly in the chair* DL)

Mike (*quietly*) Probably in the mortuary with the mother.

Rosemary (*to Leslie*) Is your father somewhere in the hospital?

Leslie Yes, he is. Mum was up here just now talking to him.

The others exchange a glance

Rosemary Talking to him?

David pulls Rosemary away

David That was before she passed on.

Mike (*whispering*) But I thought she was D.O.A.

David She was — but apparently one of the doctors gave her the kiss of life — and she came to long enough to say a few words — and then she succumbed again — permanently.

Leslie What are you lot whispering about?

David It's all right!

Hubert (*kneeling beside Leslie; gently*) Yes, it's all right. Your mother said a few final words to your father and then she very peacefully died.

David buries his head in his hands

Leslie (*blankly*) Mum died?

Hubert I think he's in shock.

David I know how he feels.

Leslie Mum spoke to Dad and died?

Rosemary Very peacefully.

Leslie (*suddenly angry*) That rotten bastard's killed my mum!

David (*backing away*) Steady, steady!

Hubert No, no, it was a number 34 bus.

Leslie He killed my mum with a number 34 bus?

David It was an accident!

Leslie Some bloody accident! The murdering swine! (*He rises and angrily breaks away*)

Mike OK, lad!

Hubert Easy now.

Mike and Hubert restrain Leslie

David (*to Rosemary*) Go and tell Matron to fill a syringe with Largactil.

Rosemary Largactil.

David Fifty milligrams. No, better make it a hundred. And get it here right away.

Rosemary hurries out through swing doors UL

Leslie I feel sick!

Mike Come on! The bathroom!

Mike and Hubert attempt to take Leslie towards the bathroom

Leslie Ignores her for eighteen years and then he hits her with a double decker.

Hubert Your father wasn't to blame.

Leslie (*wailing*) My father!

David Oh, shut up!

Hubert Steady, David.

Leslie He'd probably like to kill me, too.

David nods manically

Leslie (*to Mike*) I want to go and have it out with him.

Mike (*struggling with Leslie*) Steady! (*To Hubert*) I think we might need Dr Mortimore to give us a hand.

Hubert Good idea.

David (*calmly, cheerfully*) Dr Mortimore is on holiday.

Hubert and Mike exchange a glance

I keep telling everybody this. Nobody seems to listen. Dr Mortimore is
enjoying his Christmas break.
Mike (*to Hubert*) Is Dr Mortimore OK?
David Dr Mortimore is absolutely fine as far as I know, but he's not
prepared to work overtime and it's as simple as that.
Mike (*to Hubert*) Come on!

Hubert and Mike pull Leslie into the bathroom

Leslie (*as he goes*) How the hell did he get hold of a double decker bus?

*David closes the bathroom door as the telephone rings. David lifts the
receiver*

David (*on the phone*) Hello! . . . Nurse Tate! . . . The sergeant's coming
up here? You were supposed to be keeping him occupied. . . . No, you
stay there. (*He replaces the receiver*)

Matron enters with a large syringe on a dish

Matron Mrs Mortimore asked me to prepare a syringe for a neurotic
youth.
David Excellent.
Matron This is highly irregular. I haven't seen his medical card or
anything.
David Just do as you're told, Matron.
Matron Matron can turn ugly!
David There's no answer to that. Go on. He's in there with Dr Connolly.

*Hubert enters from the bathroom. For a moment we see Mike minister-
ing to Leslie. Hubert closes the door*

Hubert He's vomiting at the moment.
Matron Ah. (*To Hubert*) You don't think a hundred milligrams is a bit
much, Doctor?
David I'd like to give him a thousand.
Matron *A thousand?*

David Just give him the injection. A hundred milligrams won't kill him.
Hubert He's in a state of shock, you see.
David Matron doesn't need a diagnosis, Hubert.
Hubert His mother was brought in D.O.A.
Matron D.O. ——?
David (*interrupting*) Hit by a 34 bus, give him the injection, you old bat!

Matron glares at him and exits into the bathroom

(*To Hubert*) And if there's any left over, stick the rest in Matron. (*He pushes Hubert off into the bathroom*)

Hubert exits as the Sergeant enters though the door DL. He is a middle-aged man wearing the uniform of a police sergeant

Sergeant Excuse me, sir.
David Good-morning, Sergeant. Dr David Mortimore. What can I do for you?
Sergeant I'm after a young man, sir.
David Ah. A particular young man, or will anyone do?
Sergeant (*deciding to ignore this*) A particular young man, sir. Age about eighteen years, medium build, spiky haircut, wearing an earring.
David Anything distinctive about him?
Sergeant Well, he's in a bit of a state. To do with his father.
David What's his father got to do with St Andrew's, Sergeant?
Sergeant The boy has some convoluted story about his dad secretly being one of the doctors here.
David (*in mock surprise*) No!
Sergeant Yes. The mother's down at Reception, too.
David No!
Sergeant Yes. The lad wants to find his father. But from what I can gather, this medico's not keen to be found.
David Well, I certainly haven't seen a young man up here. It's been rather a quiet morning actually. But if I come across an excitable youth I'll get in touch.
Sergeant I wouldn't advise attempting to apprehend him, Doctor. He's just gone and kicked me in the goolies.
David Dear, oh dear. Anything else I can do for you, Sergeant?
Sergeant I don't think so, sir. I'll get back to Reception in case the lad's mother's got hold of him.

There is clattering from the bathroom and shouts

Matron (*off*) Keep still!
Leslie (*off*) Get away from me!
Hubert (*off*) Steady, steady!
Mike (*off*) I'm sitting on him!
Matron (*off*) That's *me*, Doctor!

    Hubert bursts in from the bathroom. For a moment we see Leslie with his trousers down, struggling with Mike and Matron. Hubert bangs the door shut

Hubert I think we need some ... (*he stops on seeing the Sergeant with David*) oh.
David (*calmly*) Sergeant, this is my colleague, Dr Bonney. How's the rehearsal going in there, Hubert?
Hubert (*after a pause*) Rehearsal?
David "Sweeney Todd" sketch, isn't it?

Hubert looks blank for a second

    Or is it "Jack the Ripper" this year? (*To the Sergeant*) Patients always like that one. "Ahoy in front and avast behind."
Matron (*off*) Take his trousers down!
David It's "Mother Goose." (*To the Sergeant*) Well, sorry I can't be of any assistance, Sergeant.
Sergeant I'll say good-morning then.
David And you said it very nicely.

David ushers out a bemused Sergeant, DL

    The Sergeant exits

Hubert I'm getting worried about you, David.
David Join the club! Go and give him the injection! (*He pushes Hubert out*)

    Hubert exits into the bathroom. Jane enters from UL

Jane Dr Mortimore!

David (*jumping*) Nurse Tate! (*Realizing*) Will you go back downstairs and keep an eye on that sergeant.

Jane I got worried about Les.

David Les is fine.

Hubert enters. For a moment we see Leslie on the window ledge being restrained by Matron and Mike. Hubert closes the door

Hubert He's climbed out through the window!

David *What?*

Jane Who has?

Hubert A young lad who's lost his mother.

Jane No!

David Hubert!

Hubert He's on the ledge, he refuses to come back in.

David (*furiously*) God!

Hubert He says he's staying out there until we bring his father to him.

Jane (*to David*) Now you'll have to tell Les.

Hubert (*bewildered*) What's the dog got to do with it?

David Hubert!

A dishevelled Matron enters from the bathroom holding the syringe

Matron Somebody send for the police.

Jane Why, what's happened?

David We don't need the police, Matron, we're perfectly capable of dealing with an unbalanced youth.

Matron He's certainly not balancing very well at the moment.

Jane I'll get that sergeant up here. (*She lifts the phone*)

David No! We don't want him again.

Jane Leslie's life's in danger. (*On the phone*) Reception please.

Hubert Has the dog had an accident?

David Shut up! (*To Jane*) It'll all come out.

Jane I'm sorry. (*To Matron*) Go and keep him talking, Matron.

Matron And who are you, madam?

Jane I'm the boy's mother.

Matron Mother?

Hubert Mother?!

David (*in mock amazement*) Oh my God!

Jane (*on the phone*) Hello?... There's a police sergeant down there somewhere. Could you send him to the Doctors' Common Room. It's an emergency. (*She replaces the receiver and moves to bathroom*)

Matron But the boy's mother was D.O.A.

Jane The boy's mother is H.E.R.E.

Jane rushes into the bathroom and Matron follows, closing the door

Hubert (*trying to take it all in*) Miss Tate is that young boy's mother?

David Hubert — I think the time has come.

Hubert What for?

David sits Hubert DL

David To confide in you. Now listen! I'm only going to say this once, Hubert. And quite fast, too. It concerns Nurse Tate.

Hubert Mrs Lesley.

David Don't interrupt, please.

Hubert Sorry.

David That's all right. Just listen. Nurse Tate *is* that young boy's mother.

Hubert But she said she had no family.

David That was a little white lie. He's her *illegitimate* son.

Hubert Illegitimate?

David She's never been married.

Hubert Never been ... what about the man who fell in the Himalayas?

David Rubbish.

Hubert What about her second husband? Mr Lesley with his gout.

David Rubbish.

Hubert And his piles.

David Piles of rubbish. She's never been married at all. The boy is a result of a liaison between Nurse Tate and a young doctor in this hospital nineteen years ago.

Hubert Good God.

David That surprises you, does it?

Hubert It certainly does.

David Well, you'd better hold very tight then. The boy's father ——

Hubert Yes?

David looks steadily at Hubert

David Is you.

Hubert takes some time trying to assimilate this

Hubert Me?

David Yes, Hubert, you.

Hubert (*protesting*) But I promise you, David. I never did anything like that with Miss Tate.

David I know you didn't, but I can't own up to it, can I, you fool.

Hubert (*pressing on*) I assure you I never touched ... (*He stops on realizing what David has just said*) *You* own up to it?

David Rosemary would make my life utter hell, the Ponsonby Lecture will go up in a puff of smoke, I would certainly kiss goodbye to being Head Physician of St Andrew's — and as for a knighthood, well!

Hubert Hang on a second. Are you telling me that you are the father of that boy through there?

David Well done, Hubert.

Hubert You mean you and Nurse Tate ——

David You've put two and two together very well, Hubert.

Hubert My whole world is turning upside down.

David Mine's not too steady either.

Hubert But the boy doesn't appear to even know you.

David All he knows is that his father was a young doctor here nineteen years ago and still works in the hospital. You fit the bill perfectly.

Hubert With one tiny exception. It wasn't me who seduced Nurse Tate.

David You would have done if you'd got half a chance.

Hubert That's beside the point.

David Hubert! It's too late for me to own up. I've already told him I'm a clergyman recovering from gout and piles.

Hubert What?

David If you're going to tell a lie, tell a whopper. Hubert, please! You've got nothing to lose.

Hubert Nothing to lose?!

David Well, you're not delivering the Ponsonby Lecture at twelve o'clock, are you?

Hubert No, but that's got nothing ——

David (*pressing on*) And you're not likely to be nominated as Head Physician here, are you?

Hubert Well, maybe not, but ——

David (*pressing on*) And you're not even in line for an American Express card, let alone a knighthood.

Hubert None of this has anything to do ... I've already got an American Express card.

David Hubert! Above all, you don't have a wife to worry about.

Hubert I've got a dippy old mother to worry about.

David A dippy old mother?! My wife's in the hospital stalking the corridor!

Hubert My mother's at home stuffing the turkey!

David If Rosemary finds out about this it'll be more than the turkey that gets stuffed.

Hubert (*breaking away* R) That's still no good reason for me to adopt your son.

David It's only for an hour or so. Simply introduce yourself to Leslie ——

Hubert What's the dog got to do with it?

David sits Hubert DR

David Forget the dog! There is no dog. The boy's name is Leslie.

Hubert Same as the fellow with gout.

David That was Mr Lesley. Only there is no Mr Lesley, Hubert! Erase Mr Lesley — and Mr Tate — and the dog — and the dead mother — and the 34 bus —— erase them all from your mind. The boy's first name is Leslie. All you have to do is to introduce yourself to him as his long-lost daddy and accompany him to the police station.

Hubert looks at David

Hubert (*flatly*) Police station?

David There's a few minor formalities concerning motoring offences.

Hubert Oh, my goodness!

David As soon as I've finished my lecture — I'll go and tell Leslie the truth.

Hubert You will?

David Of course. Piece of cake.

Hubert It's a hell of a thing to ask.

David And my letter to the hospital board will be in the post tonight.

Hubert What letter?

David Recommending you for the position of Dean of the Faculty.

Hubert (*hoarsely*) Dean of the Faculty?

David Dean of the Faculty!

Hubert That's bribery.

David Your diagnoses were always spot on. Hubert, please! I'm desperate.

Hubert (*breaking away* DL) We don't even know that Nurse Tate will agree to it.

David She'll have no alternative.

Hubert No, I'm no good at that sort of thing.

Hubert sits DL. David moves behind the chair and comes down on Hubert's left

David Nonsense. You're one of the stalwarts of the St Andrew's Operatic and Dramatic Group.

Hubert But this is for real. I'll never get away with it.

Leslie appears on the ledge outside the windows from around the corner UR, during the following dialogue. He is holding on precariously with his face pressed to the window. He gets to UL of the window

David Of course you will. It's only for half an hour at the most.

Hubert No, I really can't.

David Nothing can go wrong.

Hubert I've heard that before!

Matron, on her hands and knees, appears on the window ledge following Leslie in a similarly precarious manner during the following dialogue. She is still holding the syringe. She and Leslie start struggling with each other. Matron is attempting to jab the syringe into Leslie's backside

David You're my only chance, Hubert.

Hubert Ask Dr Connolly to do it.

Hubert rises and breaks DL, followed by David

David Don't be daft. He was about seven years old when Leslie was born.

Hubert There must be someone else you can ask?

David There's no time.

Hubert I'll have to think about it.

David There's no time. And there isn't anyone else. Only you.

Hubert Surely one of the older doctors here ——
David Hubert! There's nobody else who can help me.
Hubert (*seeing the struggling mêlée outside*) God Almighty!
David Well, he's about the only one.
Hubert (*calling*) Matron! (*He hurries to the window*)
David (*still not realizing*) Don't be daft, how could Matron be the boy's
    father? Oh, I don't know though. No, Hubert, it will have to be you. All
    you have to say is —— (*He turns and sees the drama*) Bloody hell!

*Hubert, who has got the window open, is struggling with Leslie and
Matron who are both shouting. David hurries to assist. The wind is heard
whistling and the falling snow is blown in*

Hubert Hold tight, Matron!
Matron He's got the syringe.

Leslie gets the syringe from Matron and they struggle

    Don't be silly.
Leslie Get away from me!
Matron You naughty boy!
Leslie Get away, I said. (*He sticks the syringe into Matron's backside*)
Matron Ahhh! (*She clasps her backside*)

David and Hubert step back, mortified

Leslie I told you to get away.
Matron I've been injected with a hundred milligrams of Largactil!

Mike hurries in from the bathroom and moves DR

Hubert Dr Connolly, where are you going?
Mike To get a doctor!
David Connolly, you *are* a doctor!
Mike Some other doctor!
David Why, for heaven's sake?
Mike I can't stand heights!

Mike hurries out DR *as Jane appears on ledge from around the corner*

Hubert grabs hold of Jane while David struggles with Leslie

David Nurse Tate!
Jane Leslie, darling!
Matron I'll "Leslie darling" him.
Leslie Mummy!
Jane Yes, Mummy's here. (*To David*) He went berserk.
David We can see that!
Jane What idiot told him I'd been hit by a 34 bus?
David This idiot did! (*Pulling Leslie*) Come in, you horrible boy!

Drake enters purposefully from DR

Drake (*entering*) Dr Mortimore ... !

Hubert and David, in one quick movement, pull the curtains over the window. David hurries to Drake. Hubert remains up on the window seat in front of the closed curtains

David (*charmingly*) Ah, *there* you are, Sir Willoughby!
Drake (*with studied calm*) Dr Mortimore, you are perfectly at liberty to ignore the suggestion that I could possibly be of assistance with your speech.
David Thank you, sir. No help required.
Drake (*controlling his temper*) However, it is now eleven thirty-eight. (*Or whatever the exact time is by the clock!*)
David I make it eleven thirty-seven. (*Or a minute* less *than the exact time by the clock!*)
Drake (*controlling his temper*) And the first of the delegates are starting to arrive for your lecture.
David And they're in for a good one.
Matron (*unseen on the ledge*) I'm slipping, I'm slipping!

They both turn to the window. Hubert is nonplussed

Hubert (*finally*) I'm slipping, I'm slipping!
David Well, get down then, Dr Bonney. And thanks for fixing the draught. (*Smiling at Drake*) Do allow me to get you a drink, Sir Willoughby. (*He pours a drink at the sideboard* L)
Drake Never mind a drink, Doctor. It is customary for the Ponsonby

Lecturer to welcome his fellow physicians.

Drake indicates for David to go. David gives Drake a tumbler full of whisky

David Well, I don't think I hold with that.
Drake (*hissing*) What?
David No, I'm the star of the show and I don't think I should be seen before I make my big entrance.
Drake I see!
Matron (*unseen on the ledge*) Help!

They turn to look at Hubert who is still on the window seat

Hubert Help!
David Really, Dr Bonney, you're a big boy now, jump.

Hubert smiles nervously and then jumps down. David smiles at Drake

Drake (*ominously*) So you'd like a big entrance, would you, Dr Mortimore?
David With a fanfare.
Matron (*unseen on the ledge*) You idiot!

They turn to look at Hubert

Hubert (*to Drake*) You idiot!

Drake almost explodes and then exits DR

David hurries up to Hubert and they open the curtains to see Matron and Leslie still struggling

At the same time, the door DL *opens and the Sergeant enters*

Sergeant (*entering*) Right now!

David and Hubert immediately close the curtains and David walks, smiling, down to the Sergeant, leaving Hubert on the window seat

David Good-morning again, Sergeant.

Sergeant Where's that boy? What's happened, Doctor?

David Happened? Nothing. Like I said, very slack morning so far.

Sergeant I got a message from Mrs Tate to come up here, urgent.

David Ah, yes. It *was* urgent. It isn't now.

Sergeant About her barmy young lad, wasn't it?

David Yes, no problem. His mother's persuaded him to go with her to your police station.

Sergeant West End Central?

David West End Central, yes. They left five minutes ago.

Sergeant I'll get back there right away, sir.

David Yes, you'll find him as meek as a kitten.

Matron (*unseen on the ledge*) I'm falling!

David and the Sergeant turn to look at Hubert

Hubert (*imitating Matron, singing*) "I'm falling — in love again ..." (*He continues to sing in the manner of Marlene Dietrich*) "Never wanted to — what am I to do — I can't help it."

The Sergeant looks at David who smiles and applauds politely

David Thank you, Dr Bonney. Very nice. Still rehearsing.

David takes the Sergeant's arm

Thanks for all your efforts, Sergeant. You can return to West End Central.

Leslie (*unseen on the ledge*) Mummy!

David and the Sergeant turn to the window

Hubert (*singing à la Jolson*) "Mammy! Mammy! The sun shines east, the sun shines west. I know where the sun shines best." (*He jumps off the seat and gets down on his knees*) "It's my Mammy I'm talking about. Don't you know me? I'm your little baby. I'd walk a million miles for one of your smiles. My Ma — ma — my!" (*He ends up* DC *with a big finish*)

David (*applauding*) Very good! Cliff Richard. Excellent. (*To the Sergeant*) The pantomime's on Boxing Day. Do drop in.

Sergeant Er — no thanks. Christmas is a busy time for the force. I'll get back to the station then.
David And may the force be with you.

The Sergeant exits hesitantly DL

Matron (*screaming*) Ahhh!

David and Hubert react and then rush to open the curtains. Jane, Leslie and Matron are still there but all we can see now of Matron, who has slipped off the ledge, are her head and her arms as she clings to Leslie's waist. Leslie is kneeling on the ledge holding on to the open window

Jane She slipped.
Hubert Are you all right, Matron?
David That's a bloody silly question.
Hubert Don't let go, will you, Matron?
Matron So's that!
David Hubert, get down to the floor below. See if you can grab Matron from underneath.
Hubert Right! (*He stops*) When you say grab her from underneath —— ?
David Hurry up! (*He pushes Hubert out*)

Hubert exits UL

Matron, see if you can kick in the window on the floor below.
Matron I don't think I can hold on much longer. I'm beginning to feel drowsy.
David (*looking out of the window*) Where's that idiot, Hubert?

Sister enters from UL *wheeling an old gentleman, Bill Lesley, in a wheelchair*

Sister Excuse me, Dr Mortimore ——

David hastily closes the curtains

David Yes, Sister?!
Sister Well, Matron asked me to find Mr Lesley and we've found him.
David (*confused*) Mr Lesley?

Sister Only he was in C Ward, not B Ward.
David What?!
Bill (*giving David a genial wave*) Hello.
Sister And it's not gout or piles, just old age.
David Sister! Matron is holding on by her fingertips!
Sister Well, Christmas is always hectic but she mustn't give way.
David Get out!

Sister hurries out UL

Bill is left DL. *He looks around, smiling*

Bill (*to David*) I'm going to have my own room at last, am I?
David Excuse me.
Bill (*seeing the drinks tray on the sideboard*) Oh, and you've given me a
    private bar.
David Excuse me. (*He hurries up to the window and opens the curtains*)

Bill gets out of his wheelchair and quite nimbly goes to the drinks

David (*hurrying to Matron*) Help is on its way, Matron.
Matron I want to go to sleep.
David (*shaking Matron's shoulders*) No, you don't. (*To Jane*) In the
    corridor outside there's a hose reel, quick.
Jane You're not going to hit her, are you?
David I'm going to try and pull her up. Just get it!
Leslie Don't leave me alone with the vicar.
Jane The vicar?
David Just get the hose reel!

Jane hurries out DR

Leslie (*calling*) Don't leave me, Mum!
David Shut up, you horrible boy! (*He slaps him across the back of the
    head*)
Leslie Ouch!

*Leslie lets go with one hand to hold on to his head and loses his balance
for a moment*

Matron disappears from view

Matron (*as she goes*) Ahhh!

David looks over the edge in horror. There is a pause

David (*calling*) Oh. Well caught, Hubert! ... Haul her in! ... First class!

Mike enters DR, *wheeling the trolley*

Mike We'll put Matron on ... God, where is she?
David She went over the edge.
Mike (*averting his eyes*) Oh, no!
David Dr Bonney caught her! They're on the floor below. Give them a hand.
Mike I don't know how Matron feels but I'm feeling quite queasy.

Mike exits DR *leaving trolley across the bathroom door*

David (*to Leslie*) Come on in, you.
Leslie I'm not moving until my dad gets here.
David (*furiously*) Your dad's very busy being a hero.
Leslie A hero?
David He just saved Matron.

Leslie takes this in

Leslie (*happily incredulous*) That's my father? (*He leans over the edge to have a look*)
David Yes! So you can come in now.
Leslie That funny little man's my dad?
David I told you, yes!

Leslie leans over further

Leslie (*calling down*) Dad!
David Careful!

David hauls Leslie in and shuts the windows. Leslie moves down to Bill who has just got back into his chair with a full glass of whisky

Leslie (*to Bill*) I've found my dad!

Bill looks around the room

It's amazing!

Leslie shakes Bill's hand excitedly which results in the glass in Bill's other hand shooting all the contents into the air and over his head. Leslie doesn't know whether to laugh or cry. Bill sits there pondering where the water came from

Hey, that's great. That's fantastic! (*Laughing and crying, he shakes David's hand*) Really amazing! I've found him! (*He suddenly bursts into tears and grabs David*)
Bill (*to Leslie*) Have a cuddle, I'm broadminded.
David (*to Leslie*) Come on. Let's get out of here and meet your dad downstairs.

Jane enters struggling with a fire extinguisher (red, with a short rubber nozzle)

Jane I couldn't find a hose reel.
David It doesn't matter now!
Leslie (*smiling through his tears*) Mum — I've found Dad.

Leslie is hugging David. She naturally thinks David has told Leslie the truth. She puts the fire extinguisher by the chair DR

Jane Oh, I'm so happy for you both.
Leslie Isn't it fantastic!

Leslie runs to Jane and they hug

Hubert enters

Hubert They're treating Matron for cuts and bruises.

Leslie takes a step to Hubert and points at him

Leslie My hero!

Hubert looks around to see to whom Leslie is referring. His eyes meet Bill who smiles and waves. Hubert waves back. Leslie advances on Hubert, hugs him, twirls him around and kisses him. Hubert, astonished, disentangles himself

.

Hello, Dad!

There is a brief pause and then Hubert realizes the situation. He looks furious and turns to David. David puts his hands together imploring Hubert to agree to the pretence. Music as —

— the Curtain *falls*

ACT II

The same. Immediately following

The action is continuous. NB. Stage management must stop clock during the interval!

Hubert finally reaches a decision

Hubert (*to Leslie*) Hello, son.

Hubert opens his arms and a delighted Leslie grabs Hubert

Bill I say — is my room always going to be this crowded?
Leslie Somehow I knew he'd be brave.
Jane Brave — who?
Leslie My dad. (*He hugs Hubert*)
Jane Dad? Dr Bonney?
Leslie Oh, I love that name. Bonney! (*To Hubert*) My Bonney dad!

Leslie laughs. Hubert does his best to laugh

Jane (*to David*) What the dickens have you told him?
David What Dr Bonney asked me to tell him. That he's Les's long-lost father.
Leslie And we feel fantastic, don't we, Dad.

Hubert does his best to laugh

David There we are. They feel fantastic. Now pop along to West End Central Police Station. The sergeant's waiting there for you.
Leslie (*grabbing Hubert's hand*) Come on, Dad! (*He pulls Hubert to the door* DL)
Jane (*to Hubert, across Bill*) Why don't *you* say something?
Bill I've nothing to say, madam. (*He wheels himself away*)
Jane (*to Hubert*) Say something, Hubert!

Leslie (*delighted*) Hubert! My dad's name is Hubert!

Bill My name's Bill, by the way.

Leslie Dr Hubert Bonney! (*To Hubert*) We've got so much to learn about each other, haven't we, Dad?

Hubert Oh, yes.

Jane Hubert, I just can't let you ——

David (*quickly*) Yes, you can! Can't you see how happy the boy is?

Leslie clasps Hubert

Leslie (*joyfully*) Happy's just not the word.

David (*to Jane*) You want him to be happy, don't you? Look at the pair of them! Well, look at Leslie anyway. (*He lifts the receiver and presses the button. On the phone*) Hello! Hello!

Bill (*singing*) "Who's your lady friend. Who's the little girlie by your side ..."

David glares at Bill

David (*on the phone*) Hello, Reception? Order a taxi for Dr Bonney immediately. (*To Jane*) For the moment it's for the best, I promise you.

Jane Whose best?

David Leslie's best. You don't want him to have a relapse, do you?

Jane Relapse?

Hubert It's all right!

David (*on the phone*) No, we can't wait two minutes for one. It's an emergency. And if you can't get a taxi they'll go in an ambulance. (*He replaces the receiver and collects Hubert's overcoat*)

Leslie Why should I have a relapse? (*To Hubert*) There isn't any more I should know, is there, Dad?

Hubert No, I think that's enough for one day, son.

Leslie Look, if you're worried about you, Mum and the past——

Hubert No, it's more me, Mum and the future.

David has Hubert's scarf and overcoat and, during the ensuing dialogue, he puts them on Hubert

David Dr Bonney will take you all downstairs to wait for the taxi.

Leslie (*to Hubert*) There's so much I want to know about the family, Dad. I feel like a book with the first couple of pages missing.

David The first couple of pages are always terribly dreary.

Leslie (*suddenly*) I mean, for instance, I've got a whole new set of grandparents, haven't I?

Hubert looks distraught

David Yes, your dad will tell you all about them. Off you go, Hubert.

Jane Leslie, darling ——?

Leslie Hey! I must have got cousins, too, all over the place.

David Very distant. Goodbye, everybody.

Leslie Can't you see what it means to me? Cousins! I've got their genes!

David We'll have them cleaned and sent back, just go!

Leslie puts his arms around Hubert and Jane

Leslie I want you both to know I'm very together now. I'm really, truly blissfully happy.

David There we are. We're all happy!

Bill I'm not happy.

They all look at him

Bill About sharing this room with everybody.

David (*leaning on Bill's wheelchair, to Bill*) Thank you! (*To the others*) Off you go, then.

Rosemary enters from the swing doors R

Rosemary For God's sake, David, what's happening up here?

David (*nonchalantly*) Nothing much.

David pushes Bill firmly upstage and the wheelchair hits the window seat with a jolt. David smiles politely at Rosemary

Very quiet day up till now.

Rosemary David — Matron fell out of this window!

David Oh, yes, that.

Rosemary And your lecture's due to start in fifteen minutes. (*Or however many minutes it is until 12 o'clock by the clock*)

David (*gaily*) I'm on my way. (*To Hubert*) You'll forgive me if I don't see you off.

Leslie (*to David*) And I hope your gout and piles clear up, Vicar.

Rosemary looks at David who smiles happily and looks around for an imaginary vicar

Rosemary (*to Leslie*) Haven't they found your father yet?
Leslie (*in his seventh heaven*) Oh, yes!

Leslie looks to Hubert who indicates for Leslie to be quiet

Rosemary That's a relief.
David But he can't tell you who it is.
Rosemary (*to Leslie*) Is he going to look after you?
Leslie Oh, yeah.

Leslie looks to Hubert who indicates for Leslie to be quiet

Rosemary (*to David*) But he can't tell me who it is.
Leslie No.
David No, nobody can.
Bill Yes, *I* can, it's him.

Bill points to Hubert. Rosemary looks at Hubert, amazed. Hubert nearly dies. David glares at Bill

   (*To David*) Do I get a prize?
David (*through gritted teeth*) Oh, yes, you'll get a prize.

David pushes Bill upstage with even more vigour and the wheelchair hits the window seat with an even bigger jolt

Rosemary (*bewildered*) Wait a minute! (*To Leslie*) Dr Bonney is your
   father?
Leslie I didn't say anything — but look at the profile. (*He offers his profile
   up beside Hubert's*)
Rosemary Hubert ... ?!
David (*to Rosemary*) Darling, there's a perfectly simple explanation. (*To
   Jane*) Will you take everybody to the police station, please.
Rosemary Police ——— ?
David (*interrupting*) Don't even ask, Rosemary!
Rosemary Well, don't forget to take your little basket with you.
Jane I beg your pardon?

Leslie Hey, don't talk to my mum like that.

Rosemary I shall talk to ... (*She stops*) Your mum? I thought your mum had an unfortunate accident with a number 34 bus in Camden Town.

The phone rings. David picks it up

David (*on the phone*) Hello. Hello.

Bill (*singing*) "Who's your lady friend? Who's the little girlie by your side ..."

David glares at Bill

David (*on the phone*) Yes . . . excellent. (*He bangs the phone down*) You're going in the ambulance.

Jane looks at Hubert

Hubert (*to Jane*) Well, are you ready?

Jane Are you sure, Hubert?

Hubert The sergeant's waiting for us.

Jane OK, let's go.

Rosemary What on earth's happened since I was last in here?

Jane Don't worry. (*Glaring at David*) The vicar will have an explanation for it.

Jane exits DL

Rosemary Hubert?

Hubert Don't ask me, ask the vicar.

Hubert does up his overcoat. Bill has wheeled himself DRC

Bill There's only one thing that puzzles me ...

They all look at him

The 34 bus doesn't go to Camden Town.

There is a brief pause and then David pushes Bill upstage so that once again the wheelchair hits the window seat

David Off you all go then.
Leslie (*to Hubert*) Come on, Dad. Don't hang about — slowcoach.
Hubert Hey, don't you be cheeky to your father, Leslie.

Hubert clips Leslie around the head and they exit

Rosemary I thought Leslie was the dog.
David It doesn't matter!
Bill Fancy that lad having the same name as me — Lesley.
David (*to Rosemary*) Right, let's go!
Rosemary Wait a minute. (*To Bill*) Are you Mr Lesley?
Bill Oh, yes. I hang on to that. My friends call me Bill. Do you know why?
Rosemary No.
Bill Because it's my name, madam, my name!

Rosemary considers this

  But you can call me Mr Lesley.
David Right, let's go!
Rosemary (*to David*) Wait a minute. Is that funny woman in red married
  to this gentleman?
David (*pushing Rosemary* DR) That's right.
Bill What funny woman in red?
David (*angrily*) Mrs Lesley!
Rosemary The lady who just left.
Bill Was that the wife?

Bill looks off L *where Jane exited*

Rosemary She's been visiting you this morning.
Bill Has she? I thought she walked out on me years ago.
David She came back to apologize. Come on, Rosemary.
Rosemary David, how does Dr Bonney fit into all this?
David Not very happily, Rosemary, I can tell you.
Bill I must say the little woman has worn amazingly well.
David Right, darling. Wish me luck.

Hubert hurries in, panting, from DL

What the blazes are you doing back here?

Hubert can't speak for lack of breath

Hubert, the suspense is killing me.

Hubert still can't speak

Is it bad news?

Hubert nods his head

About your son?

Hubert nods his head

(*To Rosemary*) I think you'd better tell Sir Willoughby Drake I'll be another three minutes.
Rosemary Really!
David (*piously*) I'm sorry, Rosemary, but Hubert is my dearest and oldest friend. And he's got a problem. (*He takes Rosemary to* R)
Rosemary David, they'll all be waiting for you!
David I know.
Rosemary Well, what on earth can I say to that man, Drake?
Bill (*chuckling*) Tell him the Spaniards are coming.

They all look at Bill

David It's as good as anything else. (*He pushes Rosemary out* DR)

Rosemary exits

(*To Hubert*) You're supposed to be at West End Central Police Station.
Hubert Leslie!
David (*impatiently*) What about him?
Hubert We were just about to get into the ambulance when he was grabbed by that police sergeant.
David *He's* supposed to be at the station, too.
Hubert Apparently he was on his way out of the hospital when he saw Leslie and Matron on the window ledge.
David Oh, my God.
Hubert According to the sergeant, Leslie could now be charged with attempted suicide or attempted murder — or both.
David Just so long as they get Leslie out of St Andrew's and down to that police station.
Hubert No, Leslie's being held in our security office until the sergeant's questioned Matron.

David Matron?

Hubert He's waiting for her to be released from Casualty so she can make a statement.

David Hell!

Hubert She's got a concussion and her arm's in a sling.

David God! She won't feel like helping Leslie, I can tell you.

Hubert What about me? Leslie's telling everybody down there that I'm his long-lost bonny wee daddy.

David Shut up a minute!

Hubert It will be all over the hospital that I've fathered an illegitimate son.

David Just be grateful they think you could father anything. Look, we've got to make sure that Matron isn't questioned by the sergeant.

Hubert How do we do that?

David We've got to find someone to take the *part* of Matron.

Hubert How do we do that?

David I don't know yet. I'm waiting for inspiration to strike.

Mike enters. He is now dressed as a female for the melodrama and wearing his blonde heroine wig

Mike Right. Let's get cracking on this rehearsal.

David looks from Mike to Hubert and smiles. Hubert doesn't get the implication

David I think it's struck.

Hubert (*not realizing*) What has?

Mike This business with Matron has thrown me right out of gear. She was going to be our heroine so I had to step in.

Bill (*referring to Mike*) I say, this isn't the wife, is it?

David No!

Mike I'm looking for somebody else to be the dead body now.

David (*pointing to Bill*) You can have him in a minute. (*To Mike, expansively*) Connolly, old man.

Mike Yes, sir?

David How would you like to do Dr Bonney an enormous favour ——

Mike I'm a bit rushed at the moment.

David And earn yourself a couple of hundred pounds.

Mike Not all that rushed, actually.

David You like dressing up, don't you?

Hubert (*realizing*) Oh, no!

Mike (*smiling*) Well, I fancy I'm pretty good at it.

David Pretty good? You're marvellous. Especially female parts.

Mike Well, I've fooled some of the people some of the time.

Hubert It won't work!

David Hubert! Necessity is the mother of invention. (*To Mike*) Do you know where you could get hold of a matron's outfit?

Mike Matron's outfit? Well, laundry, I suppose.

David Excellent!

Mike Are you thinking of introducing me as a sort of matron into the melodrama?

David Something like that, yes.

Mike And for this you'll give me two hundred quid?

David Plus a bonus if you pull it off. I'll meet you in the laundry in half a minute.

Mike Terrific!

Hubert You can't ask him to impersonate Matron.

David He'll be perfect. Connolly's got decidedly female features.

Hubert Yes, but predominantly male fixtures.

David Hubert!

David pushes Mike out DR and then hurries to phone and presses a button

Mike exits

Bill (*to Hubert*) Very good of you to lay on all this entertainment for the wife and me.

David (*on the phone*) Hello, Security? Dr Mortimore here. I believe you have a police sergeant in your office? . . . Could you ask him to come up to the Doctors' Common Room right away. Tell him we've arranged for Matron to be here for questioning.

Hubert (*to David*) Please, we're in enough trouble!

David Yes, tell him it's nice and private and they can relax over a Christmas drinkie. (*He replaces the receiver and removes Hubert's overcoat*) You ring Casualty and tell them to keep Matron there as long as possible.

Hubert If my mother gets to hear of this it will kill her.

David Well, nothing else has managed to polish her off. I'll fill Connolly in and send him along. Good luck, Hubert.

Hubert Thank you. What do you mean, good luck? What have *I* got to do?

David See that nothing goes wrong, for God's sake.

Hubert I'm not going to be here!

David Of course you're going to be here, you're Leslie's father. When Connolly says he was on the window ledge for a bit of Christmas fun, agree with him.

Hubert Connolly? He wasn't on the window ledge.

David He's going to be Matron, you damn fool.

Drake enters DR, *fuming*

Drake Mortimore!

David (*calmly*) Yes, Sir Willoughby?

Drake I'm waiting to introduce you, Doctor!

David We've got five minutes yet. (*Or whatever the clock says*)

Drake Get out there!

David Yes. On the way I just need to pay a little visit to the laundry.

David exits DR

Drake Much more of this and we'll all have to pay a little visit to the laundry.

Drake exits DR

Hubert presses a button on the phone

Bill (*to Hubert*) I say, isn't this fun?

Hubert glares at Bill

Hubert (*on the phone*) Hello!

Bill (*singing*) "Who's your lady friend? Who's the little girlie by your side ..."

Hubert glares at Bill

Hubert (*on the phone*) Hello, Casualty? Dr Bonney here. Is Matron still with you? ... Good. ... No, don't let her go. You keep her down there. I want her to have every available test — heart, blood, urine, bowels, the lot ... take your time. Make it thorough. 'Bye. (*He puts the phone down*)

There is a knock on the door DL

Bill Come in, come in, whoever you are.

The Sergeant enters

Sergeant Oh, I was expecting to find Matron here.
Hubert She's on her way.
Sergeant And I think maybe you should get back to that son of yours, Doctor.
Hubert Is Leslie playing up again?
Sergeant Well, his mother's coping as best she can but this could be a serious business that your lad's in.
Hubert I assure you that it's all a misunderstanding.
Sergeant Well, we'll see what your Matron has to say.
Hubert Oh, you don't have to worry about Matron.
Bill Apart from the fixtures, of course.

The Sergeant and Hubert look at Bill who smiles benignly

Hubert Mr Lesley is one of our long-term patients. Wouldn't you like to return to your ward, Mr Lesley?
Bill No, I prefer this private room any day. (*To the Sergeant*) Trouble is, my wife's turned up unexpectedly...
Sergeant Has she?
Bill And, would you believe it, there's no bed.
Hubert We'll sort it out, Mr Lesley.
Bill (*to Hubert*) She went off with you just now.
Hubert Who did?
Bill (*to the Sergeant*) They're so dense, these doctors. (*To Hubert*) My wife. You took my wife out through there just now.
Hubert Your ... ? (*Realizing*) Oh, yes! Of course, Mrs *Lesley*.
Bill (*to the Sergeant*) Dense. (*To Hubert*) You can send her back up if she's ready. She looked in pretty good nick.
Hubert No, she's waiting downstairs in our Security office. As I was saying, Sergeant ——
Sergeant (*taking Hubert aside*) Excuse me, Doctor, is the lady waiting downstairs married to this gentleman?
Hubert I think so, yes.
Sergeant I somehow assumed that because you and the lady were the boy's parents — I mean, you *are* the boy's father?

Hubert (*faintly*) Yes.

Sergeant (*referring to Bill*) So *he's* the boy's stepfather.

Hubert But I wouldn't worry him with that now.

Sergeant (*chuckling*) Well, he's certainly got himself an attractive young lady wife.

Hubert Hasn't he just.

Sergeant (*to Bill*) You've done very well for yourself, sir.

Bill And I started off at thirteen behind the counter, you know.

The Sergeant looks perplexed

Hubert (*to the Sergeant*) Mr Lesley's not always with us. Comes of marrying a younger woman.

Sergeant (*chuckling*) I thought it made you go blind. Well, I must say, the goings on at St Andrews have got *Coronation Street* beat.

Hubert Like I said, relations in this hospital are a bit confused at the moment.

Sergeant (*chuckling*) Yes, well, mine's pretty straightforward as it happens.

Hubert Your what, Sergeant?

Sergeant My relations in this hospital. My young nephew is on the staff here.

Hubert (*pleasantly*) Is that a fact now?

Sergeant You probably know him. Dr Connolly.

Hubert looks blank for a moment as his mind whirls and then he emits a nervous giggle

Hubert Dr Connolly is your nephew?

Sergeant (*chuckling*) Yeah, my brother's lad. Bit of a daft bugger.

Hubert Oh, I don't know.

Sergeant Always up to some sort of tomfoolery.

Hubert (*to the Sergeant*) Excuse me. (*He takes out his Talk-Back bleeper and presses buttons. Into the Talk-Back*) Dr Mortimore to the Common Room. Emergency, emergency, emergency.

Sergeant What's happened?

Hubert I need to contact Dr Mortimore.

Sergeant What for?

Hubert I suddenly realized we've prescribed the wrong treatment.

Sergeant The wrong treatment?

Hubert For Matron. Well, for Matron's condition. (*Into the Talk-Back*) Mayday, Mayday, Mayday!

Sergeant Dr Mortimore said something about a drink.

Hubert Yes, I suggest you have a large whisky, Sergeant.

Sergeant I'm on duty, Doctor. I'll have a small one.

Hubert A small one.

From behind the Sergeant, Mike enters DR, *dressed as Matron and wearing his heroine's wig. His arm is in a sling*

Hubert (*yelling*) No!

Hubert grabs the Sergeant to him

Mike, unseen by the Sergeant, about turns and exits DR

Hubert releases the Sergeant who is looking very surprised

No — you mustn't have a small one. Have a large one.

Sergeant (*levelly*) I'll have a small one.

Hubert Yes. (*Into the Talk-Back*) Dr Mortimore, help!

David storms in from DR

David What the hell's going on?

Hubert (*at a loss*) We've prescribed the wrong treatment. (*He flicks his finger across David, indicating the Sergeant*)

David looks down at Hubert's madly flicking finger which is in the vicinity of David's crotch. David slaps Hubert's hand

David (*bemused*) The wrong ... ?! Sir Willoughby was in the middle of introducing me to the delegates when your stupid voice came through the loudspeaker yelling, "Emergency, emergency, emergency"!

Hubert Yes. I was telling *Sergeant <u>Connolly</u>* about that, wasn't I, *Sergeant <u>Connolly</u>*?

David (*not getting the message*) You're supposed to be giving the sergeant a drink.

Hubert I *am* giving *Sergeant <u>Connolly</u>* a drink.

David Well, give the sergeant a drink then. (*He pulls Hubert across him to the drinks*)

Bill And while you're at it I wouldn't say no to a small double.

David turns Bill around and pushes him out through the swing doors UL

   Bill exits

From off we hear a loud clattering noise as Bill careers down the corridor. This noise continues for some time. David smiles at the Sergeant

David (*referring to Bill*) Isn't he sweet? (*To Hubert*) Come on then, what's the emergency, for God's sake, and where's our Matron?
Hubert Ah! Yes, that's the emergency. (*He flicks his finger across David, pointing to the Sergeant*)
David What's the matter with you, Hubert?!
Sergeant He's prescribed the wrong treatment.
Hubert That's right, *Sergeant Connolly.* Thank you, *Sergeant Connolly.* Water or soda, *Sergeant Connolly.*
David Stop shouting, Hubert.
Hubert I wasn't shouting Hubert, I was shouting Sergeant *Connolly!*

   Bill returns from UL, *smiling happily*

Bill I say!

David and Hubert collapse

   I found my own way back.

David and Hubert glare at Bill

Sergeant I'll have a splash of soda.
Hubert Soda. Right! (*He gets the syphon*)
David And I've got to go and start my lecture.
Hubert No, you've got to stay here and give Sergeant *Connolly* his soda. (*He thrusts the soda at David.*)
David (*angrily*) Say when, Sergeant.
Hubert (*shouting*) Say when, Sergeant *Connolly!*
David (*shouting*) All right, say when, Sergeant Connolly! (*Realizing, shouting*) Connolly! (*He inadvertently presses the soda syphon handle and squirts the soda into the Sergeant's lap*)
Sergeant Ah!

David I'm so sorry.
Sergeant It's OK! It's OK!
David Hubert, get a cloth.

Hubert hurries to fetch a cloth and tidies up the Sergeant

   (*To Sergeant*) I apologize.
Sergeant All right!
Hubert What a thing to do to *Dr Connolly's* <u>uncle</u>!
David Uncle!

David inadvertently squirts the soda into the Sergeant's lap once more

Sergeant For God's sake!
David I'm so sorry!
Hubert (*taking the syphon*) I think you'd better give me this.
David Good idea.
Bill Then can I have a go?

David glares at Bill

David (*mopping the Sergeant*) I can't apologize enough. I've been
   working very long hours this week.
Hubert Yes, he did six operations before breakfast.
Sergeant Did they all survive?
Hubert Jolly good! "Did they all survive?" Right now say when.

Mike returns from DR *still dressed as Matron*

David Not now!
Hubert (*jumping*) Ah!

This makes Hubert squirt soda into the Sergeant's lap

   Mike, who has not been seen by the Sergeant, about turns and exits

   I'm so sorry, Sergeant.

David grabs the syphon from Hubert and, without thinking, hands it to Bill

Sergeant (*standing up*) Bloody hell!

Hubert I do apologize. (*He sits the Sergeant*)

Both David and Hubert are mopping up the Sergeant. Bill is delightedly lining up the Sergeant so that he can have a go with the syphon

Sergeant I'll be OK.
David Dr Bonney's been working very hard recently.
Sergeant How many operations has *he* performed?

David laughs merrily

David (*laughing*) Very good! 'How many operations ...?'
Sergeant Look, how much longer is your Matron going to be?
David (*to Hubert*) Yes, where has that damn woman got to? Go and make sure she doesn't — er — doesn't — er ...

David is pushing Hubert towards the swing door R

  Mike enters again still dressed as Matron

  Get back!
Bill (*jumping*) Ah!

Bill squirts the syphon into the Sergeant's lap. At the same time, David pushes Hubert who about turns Mike

  Hubert and Mike exit DR

Sergeant God Almighty!
David I'm so sorry. (*To Bill*) That was a damn silly thing to do.
Bill Yes, great, wasn't it?
Sergeant Why the blazes is everybody shouting?
David Was I shouting?
Sergeant (*suddenly realizing*) Where's Dr Bonney gone?
David Dr Bonney? He was called away on an emergency. (*He takes out his Talk-Back*) Didn't you hear his bleeper go?
Sergeant No.
David Aren't they marvellous. They're so silent.
Sergeant (*warily*) Look, if your Matron isn't coming, I'll go and find her in Casualty.

David No, Matron *is* coming.
Sergeant *When?*
David That's a very good question. (*Dithering*) I think — er — I think — er — I think maybe I'd better go and find one — find Matron.

David hurriedly exits UL

Sergeant (*calling after him*) Dr Mortimore ——— !
Bill (*to the Sergeant*) It's all on the National Health, you know.

The Sergeant moves and sits very gingerly because of his wet trousers

Bill (*to the Sergeant, referring to the Sergeant's trousers*) It's all right, it's not an inside job.

The Sergeant looks at him woefully

Rosemary hurries in from DR

Rosemary Has anyone seen Dr Mortimore, for heaven's sake?
Bill He's probably gone for a refill.
Rosemary A refill?
Sergeant He's gone to find Matron for me.
Rosemary Matron?

Drake enters DR *furiously*

Drake What's everybody playing at in this hospital?
Bill Water sports.
Drake Where's that idiot got to?
Bill Is that the long, thin idiot or the short, bald idiot?
Rosemary There's some kind of emergency, Sir Willoughby.
Drake There certainly is. I've now delivered three versions of my introductory speech.
Rosemary Oh, dear.
Drake Not one word of the lecture yet and the delegates are already on their second coffee break.
Rosemary I'll go and keep the Junior Health Minister happy.
Drake It's not a question of *keeping* him happy but *making* him happy.
Rosemary Leave him to me.

Rosemary exits

Drake moves to follow

Bill I say, I say, I say. If the long, thin idiot doesn't turn up, I'm very good at making funny speeches.
Drake (*almost crying*) I don't believe it.

Drake exits DR

Bill (*to the Sergeant*) I liked the squirty bit best, how about you?

The Sergeant looks grim

Here, you have a go next time.

Bill offers the syphon to the Sergeant. The Sergeant ignores it and refills his glass

Well, I wonder what they've got laid on for us next.

Hubert is propelled on by Mike

This is unseen by the Sergeant whose back is to them. Hubert is now dressed as the Matron (with large bosom) plus the blonde wig and his arm in a sling. He looks extremely unhappy

Mike exits

Hubert pulls himself together and tries to get into character. The Sergeant still hasn't seen Hubert, as he is pouring his drink, but Bill reacts to Hubert and wheels himself closer to have a better look at the huge bosom. Hubert mimes for Bill to push off. Bill sits there smiling and points to the bosom. Finally Hubert gives Bill a push into the window seat

Sergeant (*turning*) Ah, you must be the matron.

Hubert nervously adopts a Scottish accent

Hubert Och ay. Yes, I'm the matron. How do you do.

Sergeant (*stepping forward*) Sergeant Connolly, West End Central ——
Hubert (*interrupting*) No, don't come too close, Sergeant. We have gangrene in the hospital.
Sergeant Oh. (*He steps back a pace*)
Hubert Yes, and I haven't had time to wash my hands this morning.

David enters UL, *dressed as Matron with his arm in a sling. David's Matron has a flat chest and a Welsh accent. He is also wearing black tights and white knickers*

David Well, where's that police ——
Hubert
          } (*seeing each other; together*) Ahhh!
David
Bill (*jumping*) Ooo!

Bill squirts the Sergeant with the soda syphon. The Sergeant mops himself. For a moment, David and Hubert are transfixed by each other, then Hubert breaks away in despair. David smiles coyly at the Sergeant

David I'm so sorry, Sergeant, "boyo". We were a wee bit surprised to see each other.
Sergeant So I noticed. Nobody told me there was going to be two matrons.
David Nobody told me either — that you'd be questioning the *other* matron. Yes. She's Ear, Nose and Throat Matron, I'm Surgical Matron. What did old Ear, Nose and Throat have to say exactly?
Hubert Well, I was about to confess.
David Ah! About the young lad on the window ledge?

David pulls Hubert across him, to the Sergeant

Hubert We were just larking around. It was a bit of a kiss and a cuddle.
Sergeant Matron, I witnessed the incident and you were struggling with the youth.
Hubert No, no. Not struggling — cuddling. I'm afraid I'd had a wee bit too much Christmas punch and it went straight to my loins.
David That's her, the drunken slut.
Sergeant I see.
Bill Excuse me but are those balloons up top? (*He points to Hubert's bosom*)

Hubert ignores this

Hubert So you won't be preferring any charges against the young man, will you, Sergeant?
Sergeant Well, I'd better have a word with the vicar first.

Hubert and David exchange a look

Hubert Vicar?
Sergeant The young lad said there was a vicar who was present during the whole episode.
Hubert (*thinking hard*) No, no, no. I don't think so. (*To David*) Have you seen a vicar, Matron Surgical?
David No, no, Ear, Nose and Throat.
Hubert }
David } (*together*) No, no, there was no vicar.
Hubert Definitely, no vicar.
Bill Yes there was, a clergyman with gout and piles.

They glare at Bill, who decides to hastily wheel himself U *into the window seat. Bill then turns, surprised*

Sergeant I won't keep the vicar a minute. He's a patient, I gather.
David You'd better go and find him, Ear, Nose and Throat.
Hubert But it's not really necessary, is it, Sergeant?
Sergeant The sooner I see the vicar, the sooner I'll be on my way.
Hubert Yes, well ...
David Well you'd better go and find him and send him in! (*He pulls Hubert across him and pushes him off* DR)

Hubert exits

Well, if Ear, Nose and Throat has explained the situation ——
Sergeant (*moving in*) I still don't understand ——
David No, don't come too close, Sergeant. I've been in the typhoid wing all morning.
Sergeant Typhoid?
David It's totally under control.
Sergeant Good.

David Although I'm not absolutely certain about the Legionnaires Disease.

Sergeant (*stepping back a pace*) Yes, well, I still don't understand what caused the pair of you to end up with your arms in a sling.

David What do you think?

Bill I think you couldn't find any balloons.

Sergeant (*to David*) You were about to tell me how you damaged your arm, Matron.

David Yes, indeed. I got that in the second session.

Sergeant The second session?

David What you witnessed on the window ledge with Ear, Nose and Throat was the first session.

Sergeant I don't quite follow ——

Bill Yes, I'm getting a bit puzzled as well.

David You be quiet. It's time for your enema.

David picks up the fire extinguisher in a threatening manner. Bill wheels himself hastily away

Sergeant Are you saying, Matron, that both you and Ear, Nose and Throat were trying to seduce the young man?

David Yes, and I saw him first as well. (*He sits seductively*)

The Sergeant writes in his notebook

Hubert is propelled on by Mike DR wearing a dressing-gown, a dog-collar and a heavily bandaged foot. He also wears thick glasses and a small, black moustache. Mike quickly exits

Hubert's vicar is Irish. David surveys Hubert and closes his eyes in anguish. The Sergeant looks up

Hubert (*finally*) Good-morning, Sergeant. Top of the morning to you — begorrah!

Sergeant Good-morning, Vicar.

Bill Come in. Join the congregation, Vicar.

Hubert I won't come too close. Both me gout and me piles are beginning to spread.

Sergeant God, this is an unhealthy hospital.

David (*rising*) Now then, Vicar——

Hubert That's me, my son — (*quickly*) my daughter.

David The sergeant wants to know if you can corroborate ——

Sergeant The sergeant can speak for himself, Matron. (*To Hubert*) Can you corroborate that the young lad had no criminal intent during the incident you witnessed on the window ledge?

Hubert Yea, verily.

David There we are.

Sergeant Right! I can close my enquiries here and take the boy down to the police station. (*He puts his notebook down to put on his hat*)

Hubert ⎱
David ⎰ (*together*) Thank you, Sergeant!

Sergeant So, perhaps, Matron, you could ask Dr Bonney to meet us in Reception.

David I'll put a call out for Dr Bonney.

Sergeant Well, make it an urgent call.

Hubert Oh, it'll be urgent all right.

Sergeant (*to Bill*) And you let Dr Bonney worry about your stepson.

Bill Oh, yes I will.

The Sergeant starts to go. Bill squirts the Sergeant's backside with the soda syphon and throws the syphon to Hubert. The Sergeant slowly turns and confronts Hubert who is looking nonplussed

Hubert Let us spray. (*He puts his hands together and closes his eyes*)

The Sergeant marches out

Hubert removes his moustache

(*To David*) I'll never forgive you for today.

Hubert puts the syphon down on the table

Mike's face appears surreptitiously through the swing doors DR

Mike Has Uncle gone?

David Connolly! Why have you never said you had an uncle in the police force?

Mike Didn't seem relevant.

David Damn fool.

The door DL *opens and the Sergeant returns*

Sergeant (*as he enters*) I left my notebook on ——

On hearing the Sergeant's voice, Hubert smacks the moustache back on, but below his lip instead of above it. At the same time, David pulls Mike to him in an embrace to prevent the Sergeant seeing his nephew's face. The Sergeant stops on seeing the Matron clutching a struggling young man

Hubert dithers for a moment and then exits through swing door R

The Sergeant shakes his head in disbelief but then returns his attention to David and Mike. He collects his notebook, goes to exit, but stops, still transfixed

Bill (*to the Sergeant, referring to David*) Matron's just starting off the third session.

The Sergeant exits DR

Mike (*to David; grinning*) That was so sudden, Dr Mortimore.
David This is no time for levity. My career's on the line here.

Rosemary enters DR

Rosemary (*as she enters*) David, the delegates are getting restless ——

At the sound of Rosemary's voice David gets down on his hands and knees and starts polishing the linoleum

Matron ...?

David scuttles away, polishing the floor

(*Moving to him*) Matron ...?

David scuttles across the floor and polishes furiously. We now see the "matron's" knickers: long, frilly and white

(*She turns to Mike*) Dr Connolly, have you seen my husband?
Mike (*hesitating momentarily*) I think he's just popped out.

Rosemary Really! Well, if you see him before I do, tell him the delegates are getting restless.

Rosemary moves to go

Hubert enters DR. *He has changed back into his suit but his trousers are still rolled up and the moustache is on his chin*

Hubert goes to David who is still on the floor. He starts to smack David's backside

Hubert Right, I'm going to the police station and then you're going to have to give me a damn good ——! (*He realizes that he's just passed Rosemary in the doorway and, totally confused, stops smacking David*)
Rosemary Hubert — ?
Bill It's all right, he's the Sheriff of Nottingham now.

Hubert hurries to the door DR

Rosemary Hubert!

Hubert exits DR

Bill Excuse me, madam. Are they balloons up top?

Rosemary exits dumbly DR

David sits up and during the ensuing dialogue he hastily removes his uniform. We see that his trousers are rolled up to the knees

David Connolly, return Mr Lesley from whence he came. I just hope my neurologists are still in the building.
Mike When do I get my two hundred quid?
David After you've returned Mr Lesley from whence he came.
Mike (*to Bill*) Off we go, then.
Bill No, I'm quite happy here. Providing the wife and I can have a double bed.
Mike You're going back to your friends in C Ward.
Bill All right. I'll take this and liven the old codgers up a bit. (*He picks up*

the soda syphon and goes to squirt David's bottom but the syphon is pointing the wrong way and Connolly gets it)

Connolly pulls Bill off. Matron enters groggily through the door DL. She has her arm in a sling

She reacts on seeing David removing the Matron's outfit

Matron (*faintly*) Good heavens ... !
David (*realizing he's still wearing the wig*) It's *me*, Matron. (*He removes the wig*)

Matron moves unsteadily to David at R

Matron Dr Mortimore, I was told there was a police sergeant waiting for me here, to make a statement.
David It's quite all right, Matron. He went away totally satisfied. You can happily return to duty. (*He moves to the mirror to tidy himself up*)
Matron I'm really not quite up to that. I feel quite drowsy. (*She sits on the chair DR*)
David You've had a hundred milligrams of Largactil.
Matron I thought it was fifty.
David Whatever. You rest there for a while.

Drake enters DR without seeing David's attire

Drake For God's sake, Mortimore, there's pandemonium going on out there.
David There you are, Sir Willoughby! (*He hastily pours a stiff drink*)
Drake Come and start your damn lecture or we'll have a riot ——

Drake stops as David approaches with his trousers rolled up. David hands Drake the drink

David "May I welcome you, my colleagues, my fellow neurologists, ladies and gentlemen ——"

David takes a deep breath and, without thinking, puts on his wig and exits DR with his trousers still rolled up

Drake is dumbfounded. He goes to follow but stops

Drake Matron, may I remind you that this Common Room is for the doctors.

Matron (*hazily*) I've had fifty or a hundred, I'm not sure which.

Drake, totally bemused, exits DR

I need air. (*She stands up, but feels giddy and leans on the back of the armchair, holding her head*)

Hubert hurries in from DL *in a panic and goes straight to Matron who has her back to him*

Hubert Quick, get that uniform off! (*He slaps her bottom*)

Matron holds her bottom in amazement

Come on! We've got no time to lose.

He takes hold of her uniform, but Matron slaps his wrist

Don't mess about, there's been all hell let loose down below ——

He tugs at Matron's knickers which fall to her ankles. Matron, horrified, turns to face Hubert. He is aghast as he sees to whom he is talking

(*Finally, into the Talk-Back*) Dr Mortimore to the Common Room!
Matron Dr Bonney! I think you owe me an explanation.
Hubert Of course.
Matron Well?
Hubert Well what?
Matron You interfered with me just now.
Hubert I know.
Matron And then you said all hell had been let loose down below.
Hubert Yes, all hell has been let loose down below — in me — down below. That's why I interfered with you.
Matron (*surprised and pleased*) Good Lord! (*She advances on Hubert*)

Hubert starts backing away around the table and Matron follows

Hubert I've been suppressing it for years. And then — suddenly — seeing you — wounded — I couldn't control myself.

Matron (*overwhelmed*) Oh — Hubert!

Hubert (*into the Talk-Back*) Bonney to Mortimore! Bonney to Mortimore!

Matron moves to him but stops on seeing David's discarded matron's outfit. She picks it up

Matron And what's my uniform doing in here?

Hubert Well — when I thought you were unobtainable — I was going to take it home — to cuddle in bed.

Matron Cuddle my uniform?

Hubert I expect you think that's foolish.

Matron No, I don't.

Hubert (*surprised*) Don't you?

Matron I think it's very — very — moving.

Hubert (*into the Talk-Back*) Help!

Matron (*yawning*) Now I really must go and have a sleep. (*She opens the door* DL)

Hubert Have several.

Matron I think it may be in order for you to tuck me in, Hubert.

Hubert You get into bed, I'll join you there! (*Quickly*) I mean, I'll be along in a moment.

Matron Oh, Hubert, Hubert, Hubert, Hubert!

Matron exits DL

Hubert (*into the Talk-Back*) Dr Mortimore! Come in, wherever you are.

David rushes in from R *and joins Hubert. He is no longer wearing the wig and his trousers are rolled down*

David Hubert!

Hubert Thank God!

David Why aren't you at the police station with Leslie?

Hubert (*relieved*) No, listen ——

David What the hell's happened? I was in the middle of my lecture and your stupid voice started shouting again!

Hubert Never mind your lecture! All hell's been let loose down in the security office.

David It was bad enough making my entrance with my trousers rolled up and wearing that wig. (*He throws the wig on the chair* DL)

Hubert It's absolute disaster.

David I know. My Ponsonby Lecture has been taken over by Sir Willoughby Drake.

Hubert And the Security Office has been taken over by my mother.

David He's actually delivering my speech. My words ... (*He stops, realizing*) Your mother?

Hubert The sergeant was just about to take Leslie and me to the police station, when my mother arrived with the Christmas puddings.

David Christmas puddings?!

Hubert For the hospital's Christmas Day party. You know she always supplies the pudding and the mince pies and the crackers ——

David (*interrupting dementedly*) Shut up, Hubert! Just get rid of her.

Hubert It's too late! She introduced herself to the sergeant who introduced her to Leslie, who thinks he's found his long-lost granny.

David (*desperately*) I've got to finish my lecture! You'll have to deal with it.

Hubert Deal with it?! Leslie's laughing and crying, the sergeant's shouting his head off and Mother's fainted.

Bill enters from UL *in his wheelchair*

Bill I say!

David Oh, no! What are *you* doing back here?

Bill I prefer it here.

David You've got to return to your ward.

Bill Certainly not. It's full of old men.

David Go away!

Hubert Never mind him. You've got to come and tell my mother the truth.

David I've got to deal with Drake.

Bill Is he still having trouble with them Spaniards?

Jane enters

Jane Dr Bonney ...!

Bill It's the wife!

Bill stands and commences to do keep-fit exercises. David shoves Bill back into his chair

Jane (*to Hubert*) The sergeant says if you're not back within two minutes he'll arrest both you *and* Leslie.

Hubert What about my mother?!

Jane She's having a cup of tea.

Hubert A cup of tea?

Bill (*rising*) Lovely. Just as it comes for me.

Hubert Mr Lesley, will you please go!

Bill I went this morning.

David Well, go again now. It's through there! (*He pushes Bill into the bathroom*)

Bill exits

Hubert (*to Jane*) Is Mother all right?

Jane Yes, fine. She and Leslie are getting on like a house on fire.

David Great. I can get back to my lecture.

Hubert No, you've got to come and tell Leslie and my mother who Leslie's father is.

David They *know* who his father is, it's *you* and they think it's great.

Hubert No! I can't go on!

Jane Dr Bonney, please. You must.

David Yes, you must!

Jane This just isn't the time to break it to Leslie. He's only just found you.

Hubert But there's my mother now as well as the police.

Jane Hubert — Don't think I'm ungrateful for what you've already done. You've been magnificent. More than magnificent.

Hubert (*pleased but embarrassed*) Well, I did what I had to do.

Jane You've been a revelation to me.

Hubert Have I?

Jane In fact, you've touched me here. (*She puts a hand to her heart*)

David You don't hang around, do you?

Leslie enters from DL

Leslie Look out, everybody!

David What are you doing back here?

Leslie I'm being chased by that ruddy sergeant.

Hubert Why?

Leslie And Matron.

David (*aghast*) Matron?

Hubert She's supposed to be waiting for me in bed.

David goes to speak to Leslie but then realizes what Hubert has said

David (*to Hubert*) You're having a hell of a morning, aren't you?!
Hubert Never mind that. (*To Leslie*) What happened?
Leslie Well, in the first place, Matron turned up in the Security Office.
Hubert Oh, no!
David And what happened in the second place?
Leslie Well, when Matron said she was the one who was pushed off the window ledge, the sergeant seemed to hit the roof.
Hubert I can imagine that.
Leslie Then he said he's coming back up here to question the other two matrons again.
David Oh, no!
Hubert *What?*
Leslie And he'll probably arrest me for attempted murder.
Jane Poor baby.
David *Poor baby?* (*To Leslie*) You go up to the top floor (*opening the door* DL) and hide in the — Mrs Bonney!!

Mrs Bonney walks through the door. She is about eighty, small but energetic. She is heavily laden with Christmas shopping

Mother Where's Hubert?
Hubert Mother! You shouldn't be up here.
Mother Nonsense. If young Les is in a spot of bother with the police, he needs his grandmother.
Hubert Mother, things are not what they seem.
Mother I know. I didn't think you had it in you, Hubert.
Hubert Mother — !
Mother (*referring to Jane*) And I'm so pleased it was a nice girl like Nurse Tate.
Jane Thank you.
David I hate to interrupt the family gathering — (*he opens the door* DL) — but if Matron and the sergeant find Leslie ... (*He sees something in the corridor*) Oh, my God! (*He slams the door closed*) Matron and the sergeant getting out of the lift.
Hubert Oh, my God!

Bill enters from the bathroom

Bill Do you know, I wasn't able to go?

Hubert and David react

David Get back in there!
Bill (*seeing Mother*) Ah now, don't tell me. It's Mother Goose!

David and Hubert throw their hands up in despair

Mother Don't be cheeky, I'm Dr Bonney's mother.

There is a knock on the door DL. *They all react. David holds the door*

David (*calling out*) One moment, Sergeant! Nurse Tate, get Mr Leslie
  back in the bathroom.
Hubert And, Nurse Tate, take Mother with you!
Mother I don't want to go to the bathroom, Hubert.
Hubert You'll put your foot in it! (*He pushes Mother into the bathroom*)

  Mother exits

  (*To Bill*) You get in there with Mother.
Bill Yes. Is she a real mother or a balloons-up-top mother?
Hubert (*to Bill*) Get in there! (*He pushes Bill in*)

  Bill exits

There is a knock on the door. David is still holding the door

David (*calling*) One moment, Sergeant!
Sergeant (*off*) Dr Mortimore!
David (*calling*) There's nobody in ! (*Referring to Leslie*) Get rid of him,
  Hubert!

David leaves the door and it opens

  *The Sergeant enters, supporting Matron, who is now drowsy but
  fighting it*

Hubert, Jane and David, in one deft movement, lay Leslie on the trolley UC
and cover him with the sheet

Sergeant (*as they enter*) We'll soon get to the bottom of this, Matron.
Matron Well, I can assure you that there aren't any other matrons in this
  hospital.

The Sergeant sits Matron in the chair DL. *Hubert and Jane are just about*
to push the trolley off R *when the Sergeant turns*

Sergeant Oy!

They stop and look at the Sergeant who joins them C

  Where's that son of yours, Dr Bonney?
Jane (*quickly*) He's just this second gone back to the Security Office,
  Sergeant.

Jane, David and Hubert point UL

Matron Who's that? (*She points to the body*)
David (*taking a breath*) Who is it, Dr Bonney?
Hubert (*after a pause*) It's poor old Mr Lesley.

Jane wails

Hubert There, there.
Sergeant Mr Lesley?
Hubert Yes. (*Going to push trolley*) Excuse me.
Sergeant (*stopping the trolley*) You mean the old boy who was sitting in
  that wheelchair just now?
Hubert The very same. Excuse me.
Sergeant Hang on! He was bouncing up and down five minutes ago.
David Yes, that's what gave him the cardiac arrest.
Jane (*sobbing loudly*) Ohhhh!
Sergeant Poor old fellow.

The Sergeant lifts the sheet to look at the body's head, but Jane wails and
David quickly pulls the sheet down again

David Mrs Lesley has taken it very badly, hasn't she, Dr Bonney?
Hubert Not surprising, is it? Her husband came in for gout, we operated
  for piles and now he's dropped dead with a heart attack.
Jane (*wailing*) Ohhh!
Matron (*who has been nodding off, sitting up*) Yes! Matron's here.
Sergeant Ah. Right then, Matron.

*The Sergeant takes out his notebook. During the ensuing scene Matron
falls asleep*

David (*to Hubert*) I'm sure Mrs Lesley would like to accompany you
  down to the mortuary.

Leslie, under the sheet, sits up in horror

Hubert } (*together*) Down!
David }

The Sergeant turns

David To the mortuary.
Jane Thank you.
Hubert There, there.
Sergeant Just a minute! (*To David*) One of the other doctors can take Mr
  Lesley to the mortuary. I want you and Dr Bonney to answer a few more
  questions about Matron and his son.

  *During the above speech and behind the Sergeant's back Bill walks out
  of the bathroom*

Hubert neatly turns him about and shoves him back in

  Bill exits

*Hubert slams the door, leans nonchalantly against it and smiles reassur-
ingly as the Sergeant turns round. There is the sound of a long series of
glass crashes as Bill stumbles around the bathroom. The crashes cease
and Hubert opens the door an inch*

Hubert (*calling into the bathroom*) You naughty pussy! (*He shuts the
  door and leans against it*)

Sergeant Right then, Doctor Mortimore ——

The bathroom door is pushed by Bill, which gooses Hubert

Hubert Ah!

The Sergeant turns as Hubert quickly pretends that his "Ah" is the beginning of a karate exercise

Ah! Oo! Wah-ha! Ha-wha!

The Sergeant is watching in amazement

Behind Hubert and, unseen by him, Mother comes out of the bathroom

Hubert turns to come face to face with Mother. After a moment he looks back to the Sergeant

You've met Pussy, haven't you?

Hubert takes Mother to the Sergeant

Bill tries to get out of the bathroom door once more and gooses Jane

Jane Ah!

The Sergeant turns quickly and Jane goes into her karate routine

Ah! Oo! Wah-ha! Ha-wah!
Hubert Ah! Oo! Wah-ha! Ha-wah!

They go into a protracted fight

David Thank you, Doctor Bonney! I think you've both perfected that now.

Hubert and Jane finish by bowing to one another

Just put Mr Lesley in the corridor.
Hubert I was wondering if I shouldn't spend a penny first. (*He indicates the bathroom*)

Bill appears on the ledge outside the window and, during the ensuing dialogue, walks precariously along the ledge

Sergeant Nobody's spending a penny! Not you, not you, not you, not you.

David and Hubert see Bill on the window ledge

Hubert }
David }   (*together*) Ah!

The Sergeant looks at Hubert who goes into his karate routine with David

Hubert Ah! Oo! Wah-ha! Ha-wah!

David hits Matron who slips to the floor

> *Finally, miming the urgency to spend a penny, Hubert rushes into the bathroom*

Sergeant Oi!

Hubert has gone into the bathroom

> Right. Let's get some sense out of somebody. Matron!

Matron snores. During the next few lines David indicates for Jane to take the trolley off UL

> *Jane exits*

David bundles Mother out after Jane

> *Mother exits*

> Matron!
Matron (*coming to*) Yes, I'm fine now, fine.
David And she'll be even more fine tomorrow.

> *Bill appears outside the windows clutching the drainpipe which is at an angle having come away from the wall*

Sergeant Matron. If I could have your undivided attention.
Matron (*sitting up against the chair*) Of course.

Sergeant Thank you.

During the ensuing dialogue, Hubert appears outside the window

Bill gets in through the L *window and Hubert through the* R *window. Hubert grabs Bill and stuffs him in the window seat during the following*

Matron ——

He sees that she's asleep again

Matron! Matron!
Matron (*coming to*) Yes, Sergeant.
Sergeant Can you confirm that you are the only matron employed in this hospital?

Matron is already asleep again

David She's in no fit state to be questioned.
Sergeant Matron!

Matron snores

Sergeant God help us all.
David (*jovially*) Well, it looks as though you'll have to continue this after Christmas, Sergeant.

By now Bill is in the window seat and Hubert bangs the lid shut. The Sergeant turns and Hubert goes into a tap-routine

David Very good. Fred Astaire.

David applauds and Hubert bows

Sergeant God! (*Shaking Matron*) Matron!

Matron takes his hand

Matron I'm all yours, Hubert.

Sergeant *Hubert?*

David Well, Sergeant. I don't think you're going to get much sense out of Matron.

Sergeant I haven't had much sense out of anyone in this place.

David I resent that, Sergeant.

Sergeant Especially you two gentlemen.

David Us?

Hubert Us?

Sergeant It seems to me that if anyone should know how many matrons you have here, it's you two.

David We *do* know. There are three matrons: Ear, Nose and Throat; Surgical; and Pathological.

Sergeant (*pointing to Matron*) She seems to think there's only one matron.

David She would. She's pathological.

The Sergeant does not look pleased with this explanation and is about to argue

Bill appears from out of the window seat wearing the Pirate's outfit we've seen in Act I

Hubert and David nearly die. The Sergeant advances upon Bill

Bill pauses a fraction of a second, then holds one leg and hops out DR

The Sergeant looks at David and Hubert who try to smile

Sergeant (*calmly*) I suppose Mr Lesley will be walking on water next, will he?

Drake enters very deliberately from DR. He is carrying David's speech

Drake Doctor Mortimore!

Sergeant (*to Drake*) And *you* might have some explaining to do, as well. (*Shouting off*) Oi, come back here!

The Sergeant exits DR

Drake looks after the departing Sergeant and then back to David and

Hubert. Hubert sits forlornly on the arm of the chair DL, *beside Matron*

Drake What the blazes is going on in here?

David (*brightly*) I told you it was another emergency, Sir Willoughby. Matron suffered a collapse. She has these fits.

Drake (*flatly*) Matron has fits?

David And "starts". Brought on by overwork.

Drake Has Dr Bonney also suffered a collapse?

Hubert Yes, brought on by Dr Mortimore.

Drake Well, you might like to know, Mortimore, that, in your absence, I have concluded your Ponsonby Lecture for you.

David I'm abjectly sorry, Sir Willoughby.

Drake Yes — (*he beams*) — and I must say I enjoyed myself enormously.

David I can't apologize ... (*He stops*) You did?

Drake Yes. An excellent speech of yours, Mortimore — David — Sir David! (*He hands David the speech*)

David (*delighted*) Oh. Well, thank you, sir. Have another drink? (*He goes to pour whisky*)

Drake Why not?! And you were right about your entrance, too, weren't you? Really made the delegates sit up. And the Junior Health Minister! Rolled up trousers and a funny wig. (*Suddenly*) I think I'll try that with my closing speech for the delegates! (*Pulling up his trouser bottoms*) Rolled up trousers, very good. (*He sees David's matron wig on the chair*) And a funny wig!

He sticks the wig on his head and takes the proferred glass of whisky from David

Thank you. Cheers! My first today. (*As he goes*) Fellow delegates from all over the world. I would like to thank you from the heart of my bottom ...

Drake exits DR

David Hubert, we're approaching the last hurdle.

Bill runs in from UL

Bill (*breathlessly*) I'm being chased by that police sergeant.

David (*to Bill*) You were supposed to be dead.

Bill Much more of this and I will be. (*Referring to Matron*) Has she kicked the bucket, as well?

David No! You get in the bathroom.

Bill I've had half the morning in there.

David Lovely. Have the *other* half.

David pushes Bill into the bathroom then collects the wheelchair

Bill exits

Hubert (*pulling Matron up*) Matron, Matron!

David Hubert, we have to make sure that Matron isn't questioned by Sergeant Connolly. Come on, Hubert, give us a hand, what are friends for?

Hubert assists David to put Matron into the wheelchair. They inadvertently put her upside down with her legs in the air

Hubert (*helping with Matron*) I haven't noticed much friendship so far today.

Rosemary enters from DR

Rosemary David, darling.

David Rosemary!

Rosemary Sir Willoughby was absolutely thrilled with ... (*She stops on seeing Matron*) Good Lord! What's Matron doing upside down in a wheelchair!

David No trick questions, please!

Leslie and Mother enter from the DL door

Leslie Hey, Dad —— !

David Why can't you keep out of the way for five minutes?

Hubert And, Mother, will you please go home!

Rosemary Mrs Bonney, how nice to see you. What are you doing in the hospital?

David (*interrupting*) Just stick to "How nice to see you", please.

Hubert Mother, it's your tea-time.

Mother Les is more important than tea.

Leslie I just wanted you to know, Dad, that you needn't come with me to the police station.

Hubert I needn't?

Leslie No. Granny's coming with me instead.

Hubert Mother! You mustn't get involved.

David No, Mrs Bonney, you mustn't get involved!

Mike enters from DR

Mike I don't know who knows what and who doesn't know what. But I think that you *all* ought to know that Uncle Tom is heading this way looking for Mr Lesley.

Mother Uncle Tom?

Rosemary Who's Uncle Tom?

David Never mind, he's one of the bad guys. (*To Mike*) You go and dump Matron somewhere.

Mike (*pushing Matron off*) Come on, Matron.

Mike and Matron exit UL

The Sergeant enters running from DR

David Ah, Sergeant!

Sergeant Right! Where's Mr Lesley?

Jane rushes in from DL

Jane The sergeant's rampaging about looking for ... ! (*She stops on seeing the Sergeant*)

Sergeant Lovely, they're all here now. (*To Jane*) I was just asking about Mr Lesley.

Jane (*wailing*) Ahhhh!

Sergeant (*coldly*) You might like to know, madam that I've just been chasing your late husband up and down the hospital corridors — and your late husband was doing at least twenty miles per hour.

Jane Oh — it's a miracle!

Sergeant Don't give me that!

Rosemary Sergeant, really. Chasing an old man like that. You could give him a heart attack.

Sergeant Oh, he survives those all right.

Mother (*to Jane*) My dear. You're not married to Mr Lesley, are you?

Hubert Mother! Wait downstairs!

David And take your grandson with you!

Rosemary I must say, Mrs Bonney, I think it's marvellous that you haven't let the news about Leslie upset you.

Mother Well, I was a bit surprised at first.

Leslie The only person we've got to break it really gently to is Dr Bonney's wife.

Everybody looks at Leslie

Mother (*amazed*) Hubert's wife?

Leslie It's all right, Gran. Mum explained to me that my father was a married man.

Hubert and David close their eyes in anguish

Rosemary Dr Bonney!

Sergeant Which one of you lot is going to tell me the end of this fairy tale?

Mother Hubert, you haven't been covering up a wife as well, have you?

Hubert I've lost track of what I've been covering up.

Leslie I think the sooner you introduce me to your wife, the better, Dad.

Hubert (*determinedly*) There's no need to introduce you to my wife!

David (*warningly*) Hubert!

Leslie Yes there is, Dad!

Hubert No, there isn't, Leslie!

Leslie Why not?!

David (*stepping in*) Because they're divorced.

Hubert looks at David in disbelief and sinks into the chair

Mother Divorced?

David It was a quickie.

Rosemary Good God.

David Yes, they don't call him Speedy Gonzales for nothing.

Leslie That's great! (*To Hubert*) There's nothing to stop me seeing you and Gran every day now! Has this been the best day of your life, Dad?

Hubert can only look at Leslie and cry

David Well, Sergeant, as none of this involves my wife, I think she'd like
to go home.

Sergeant Your wife can go home, Doctor, when I've had some answers
to a few questions. Like why Matron Pathological had a six-inch syringe
stuck in her backside and why Ear, Nose and Throat and Surgical,
having suffered similar injections, have disappeared off the face of the
earth. Why Dr Bonney has a wife he knows nothing about, a mistress he
calls Miss Tate, Mrs Tate and Mrs Lesley — and a *mother* he calls *Pussy*.
Why the doctors in this place can make some patients rise amazingly
from the dead, and, at the same time, they don't know if *other* patients
are D.O.A., C.O.D., or have been hit by a number 34 B-U-S. Why there
seems to be some permanent pantomime rehearsal in progress running
concurrent with some vicar's tea party. Why the name Lesley seems to
cover all forms of life — from unbalanced punks to neurotic dogs. And
why, if you're called Lesley or Tate all your relatives have suffered fatal
climbing accidents in the Himalayas. Why, if you have those aforemen-
tioned names of Lesley or Tate you don't seem to know who your
mother or father is — and why I'm beginning to think you're *all* a bunch
of baskets.

There is a pause

David What was the first question again, Sergeant?

Bill enters from the bathroom and walks down to the Sergeant

Bill (*to the Sergeant*) Is it safe to come out? (*He realizes he's talking to the
Sergeant. Politely*) Nice to see you again, Sergeant.

There is a momentary pause and then Bill runs back into the bathroom

Sergeant Oi!

The Sergeant runs into the bathroom after Bill

*David quickly closes the door and puts the chair from the desk underneath
the door handle*

David Rosemary — I've got to be quick. I think the time has come to tell
you the truth about Leslie.

Jane Dr Mortimore ——
Mother We *know* the truth about Leslie.
David (*to Jane*) We can't keep it up any longer. Rosemary, prepare
    yourself for a shock ——
Rosemary David, what is it?
David This young man ——

*Before he is able to continue, the bathroom door rattles and there is a
knock*

Sergeant (*off*) Hey! Open the door!
David It's stuck, Sergeant. Hang on a second. (*To Rosemary*) This young
    man's father, Rosemary, is ——
Leslie (*interrupting*) He's the greatest, that's who my dad is. (*He hugs
    Hubert*)
David This young man ——
Rosemary Yes!
David — is mine.
Rosemary (*blankly*) Yours?
Mother (*blankly*) Yours?

There is a knocking at the bathroom door

Sergeant (*off*) What's going on out there?
David (*calling*) We've just sent for Maintenance.
Rosemary When you say yours ... ?
David Mine and Nurse Tate's.
Rosemary When you say yours and Nurse Tate's ... ?
David Don't blame her. I was young, handsome and virile.
Rosemary Are you telling me ... ?
David I'm telling you she couldn't help herself.
Rosemary But you did.

David reacts. There is more banging at the door

Sergeant (*off*) Open this door immediately!!
David (*calling*) Maintenance is on the way.
Leslie (*to David*) What are you trying to pull?
David Pull?
Leslie My mum wouldn't have an affair with the vicar.

Rosemary Affair with the vicar?

David It was nineteen years ago, Rosemary.

Leslie Even when you were a curate she wouldn't have fallen for you. (*To Jane*) Dr Bonney's my dad, isn't he? (*He hugs Hubert*)

Jane Leslie ——

Leslie (*pressing on*) He's good and kind and sensitive and thoughtful and generous and loveable and he's a hero. (*To David*) You're a pompous twit.

David *A pompous twit?*

Leslie I don't even look like you.

David Thank God for that.

Leslie You couldn't be my dad.

David I wish I wasn't but I bloody well am.

There is renewed banging on the door

Sergeant (*off*) Open this door!!!

Leslie suddenly bursts into tears. Mother, Jane and Hubert comfort him as Leslie flings himself into the chair DL

Mother Leslie!

Jane Leslie, darling.

Mother Les, you mustn't.

Hubert Leslie, don't, please.

David I've never seen anyone like him for tantrums.

Rosemary (*pointedly*) I have.

David reacts. There is more banging on the bathroom door

Sergeant (*off*) Hey!

Leslie Tell me he's lying, Mum!

Jane Leslie ——

Leslie Tell me he's lying, I've found my dad, haven't I? Dr Bonney?!

Leslie pulls a surprised Hubert on to his lap

Jane Son —— !

Leslie It's got to be Dr Bonney!

Hubert Yes, you're right, Leslie, of course it's me!

Everyone turns to look at Hubert. Hubert looks surprised at himself

(*Bravely continuing, to Jane*) Much better to stick to the truth, my dear.
Jane What?

Hubert rises and goes to David

Hubert Thanks very much, David, but there's no need to take on my responsibilities.
David (*bemused*) Isn't there?
Hubert No.
Leslie I knew it!
Mother So did I!
Leslie (*hugging Hubert*) My dad doesn't tell lies, do you, Dad?
Hubert Certainly not. (*To David*) I appreciate what you tried to do. But I assure you — I can cope. And I'm very happy with the situation as it is.
David (*floundering*) Well, if you're happy, Hubert.
Hubert I am.
David And if Nurse Tate is happy.
Jane She is!
Mother And I'm happy!
David I just thought I was in a better position to provide for the boy, that's all.
Hubert It was a very unselfish gesture on your part.
Rosemary Yes, quite unlike you, David.
David (*expansively*) Well, I thought I ought to try and help out old Hubert.
Leslie We don't need the vicar's money, do we?
Jane Definitely not.
Hubert Well, a small donation wouldn't come amiss actually. (*He smiles at David*)

There is renewed banging on the bathroom door

Sergeant (*off*) If you don't open this door I'm going to break it down.
Hubert (*calling*) We're still discussing maintenance!

As Hubert says "maintenance" he grins at David who reacts and then smiles himself

David Well, yes! I don't see why I shouldn't be a sort of uncle to the boy.

Hubert (*to Jane*) Right. I think it's all down to the police station and then back to our place for a cup of tea, Mother. (*He goes to collect his overcoat, etc.*)

Leslie Great!

Mother Oo, I make a nice cup of tea, Les.

Leslie Come on, Gran!

Leslie takes Mother off DL

Hubert Right. Thanks, David! (*To Jane*) After you — Mrs Bonney.

Jane Hubert, is that a proposal?

Hubert I missed out nineteen years ago, I'd be a fool to make the same mistake twice.

Hubert offers Jane his arm and they exit DL

David smiles politely at Rosemary who smiles politely back

Rosemary I think you've got some explaining to do — your Reverence.

David Let's go and mingle with the delegates first.

David moves Rosemary to go, but she stops

Rosemary David, that boy's eyes are brown.

David So what?

Rosemary Hubert's are blue. So are Nurse Tate's. Impossible to have a baby with brown eyes.

David (*averting his eyes*) Oh, I think there are medical exceptions.

Rosemary And the boy's wide mouth ——

David (*narrowing his lips*) I can't say I noticed that.

Rosemary And he's so devastatingly good-looking.

David (*pleased*) Do you think so? (*Off-hand*) Well — not particularly, was he?

Rosemary David — it's reassuring to know you were human, once.

David (*taking this in*) What do you mean "once"?

Rosemary You've become very stodgy lately.

David Stodgy, me?

Rosemary You were much less dreary when you used to have the odd affair.

David That's a terrible thing to say!

Rosemary You stopped about ten years ago, didn't you?

David (*blustering*) Well, I'm not sure ——

Rosemary I am. That's when you went off the boil with me, too.

David Off the boil?

Rosemary Mind you, I'm not suggesting for one minute you return to the old days in the Sluice Room.

David Rosemary!

Rosemary But a little bit more activity at home would do us both the power of good.

She kisses a surprised David

Let's go and mingle with the delegates.

David (*smiling*) I've obviously been a very lucky man, Rosemary.

Rosemary And I've been a very lucky woman, darling.

David (*still smiling*) No.

Rosemary Yes. What do you think Dr Bonney and I were up to all those evenings you were rolling around the Sluice Room?

Rosemary exits DR

David's smile slowly fades as he takes in the implication of Rosemary's remark

David (*calling*) Rosemary!

David storms out after Rosemary

Music

CURTAIN

FURNITURE AND PROPERTY LIST

ACT I

On stage: Desk. *On it*: 3 page speech, pen, **David**'s spectacles, telephone

Chair. *On back*: **David**'s jacket

Sideboard. *On it*: tray with jug of water, whisky decanter, 6 tumblers, 2 soda syphons, cloth. *In it*: dressing (trophies, urns). *Above it*: mirror on wall

2 armchairs

Christmas tree

Window seat. *In it*: fairy costume and wand, Father Christmas hat, ladies' bonnet, cowboy hat, pirate coat and hat, eye patch, pillow, Victorian pantomime dress

Curtains open at windows

Coat hooks. *On them*: **Hubert**'s hat, **Hubert**'s mac and scarf, **Hubert**'s jacket with handkerchief in top pocket

Wall clock (practical) set at 10.45

Off stage: Snow (**Stage Management**)

Plate of mince pies (**Mike**)

Trolley with wrapped presents covered in sheet (**Matron**)

Empty whisky glass (**Drake**)

Clipboard with list of presents (**Sister**)

Plate with one mince pie (**Mike**)

Kidney dish and syringe (**Matron**)

Wheelchair (**Sister**)

Red fire extinguisher (**Jane**)

Personal: **David**: bleeper, wrist-watch

Mike: 2 £1 coins in pocket, name badge on coat

Rosemary: handbag, car keys

Hubert: stethoscope, bleeper, pen and name badge in white coat, wrist-watch

Matron: nurse's watch, name badge
Jane: handbag containing handkerchief
Leslie: handkerchief, earring
Sergeant: notebook and pencil
Sister: nurse's watch, name badge
Mother: handbag

ACT II

Check: Clock set as at end of Act I

Off stage: Christmas-style shopping bags (**Mother**)
              3 page speech (**Drake**)

Personal: **Mother**: handbag

LIGHTING PLOT

Property fittings required: nil

Interior. The same scene throughout

ACT I

To open: Full general lighting

No cues

ACT II

To open: Full general lighting

No cues

EFFECTS PLOT

ACT I

Cue 1   **David:** "... such a fuss."   (Page 20)
Phone

Cue 2   **David** starts to move DR   (Page 23)
Phone

Cue 3   **David** closes the bathroom door   (Page 32)
Phone

Cue 4   **Sergeant:** "... got hold of him."   (Page 33)
Clattering and glass crash

Cue 5   **Hubert** opens the window   (Page 40)
Wind whistles, snow effect

Cue 6   **Hubert** and **David** pull the curtains   (Page 41)
Cut wind and snow effect

Cue 7   **Hubert** and **David** open the curtains   (Page 42)
Wind whistles, snow effect

Cue 8   **Hubert** and **David** close the curtains   (Page 42)
Cut wind and snow effect

Cue 9   **Hubert** and **David** open the curtains   (Page 44)
Wind whistles, snow effect

Cue 10   **David** closes the curtains   (Page 44)
Cut wind and snow effect

Cue 11	**David** open the curtains *Wind whistles, snow effect*	(Page 45)
Cue 12	**David** shuts the window *Cut wind and snow effect*	(Page 46)
Cue 13	As the CURTAIN falls *Music*	(Page 48)

ACT II

Cue 14	**Rosemary:** "... in Camden Town." *Phone*	(Page 53)
Cue 15	**Bill** exits *Clattering noise*	(Page 62)
Cue 16	**Hubert** leans against the bathroom door *Long series of glass crashes*	(Page 81)
Cue 17	**David** storms out after **Rosemary** *Music*	(Page 95)

PRINTED IN GREAT BRITAIN BY
THE LONGDUNN PRESS LTD BRISTOL
MADE IN ENGLAND